STRAIGHT ARROW's

Manual of Indian Lore

BOOK 2

STRAIGHT ARROW's

Manual of Indian Lore

BOOK 2

GEORGE FRANGOULIS

The Farmstead Press

STRAIGHT ARROW's
Manual of Indian Lore
BOOK 2

Copyright 2014 by George Frangoulis.

All rights reserved. No part of this book may be transmitted or reproduced in any form by any means without permission in writing from the publisher.

Printed in the United States of America. First printing, 2014.

ISBN: 978-1-312-38869-7
George Frangoulis
715 Canyon Rd. N.
Tuscaloosa, AL 35406

STRAIGHT ARROW
INJUN-UITY MANUAL

BOOK 2
Set of 36 INJUN-UITIES

STRAIGHT ARROW

INJUN-UITY INDEX

Subject	Page No.
Cover for Book No. 2	37
Table of Contents	38
Indian Leather Craft I	39
Indian Leather Craft II	40
Indian Moccasins I	41
Indian Moccasins II	42
Indian Spurs	43
Indian Armlets	44
Indian Belt	45
Indian Chops	46
Comanche War Bonnet	47
Blanket Roll and Pack	48
Woodsmanship	49
Indian Bull Shield	50
Indian Lance	51
Indian Snow Shoes	52
Indian Sled	53
Indian Lariat	54
Indian Hammock	55
Indian Couch	56
Pow-Wow Lodge or Canoe Shelter	57
Indian Gates	58
Canoemanship	59
Canoe Carry	60
Indian Pottery and Utensils	61
Indian Kiln	62
Aerial Bird Diner	63
Bird Shelter & Weather Vane	64
Weather Vane	65
Animal Trap (Portable)	66
Animal Trap (Stationary)	67
Archery Target - Part I	68
Archery Target - Part II	69
Height Measurements	70
Sun and Watch Compass	71
Indian Smoke Signals	72

Caution in the woods comes naturally to Indians. You must practice it, too. Experience in the outdoors is the best teacher. Always try to be prepared to meet any possible situation. Think before you act. You'll find it pays!

Like Book One,- Straight Arrow's Injunuity Manual- BOOK TWO will help you be resourceful in the woods, in open country, at home, in school, in play, and at work.

*This manual was prepared for NABISCO SHREDDED WHEAT by Fred L. Meagher, illustrator and Indian authority."

INDIAN LEATHER CRAFT I

Indians depended on leather for many of their needs. They were adept at leather craft. Below are some of their simple methods.

FLUSH LACING
To attach two pieces of material.

LAP LACING
To attach two pieces of material.

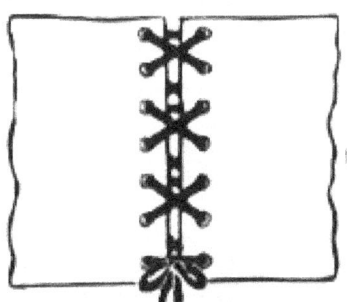 

LEATHER THONGS

Punch holes and lace as you would your shoes.

Lap the two pieces of material, punch holes, and lace as shown.

THE FAMOUS INDIAN CONCHA

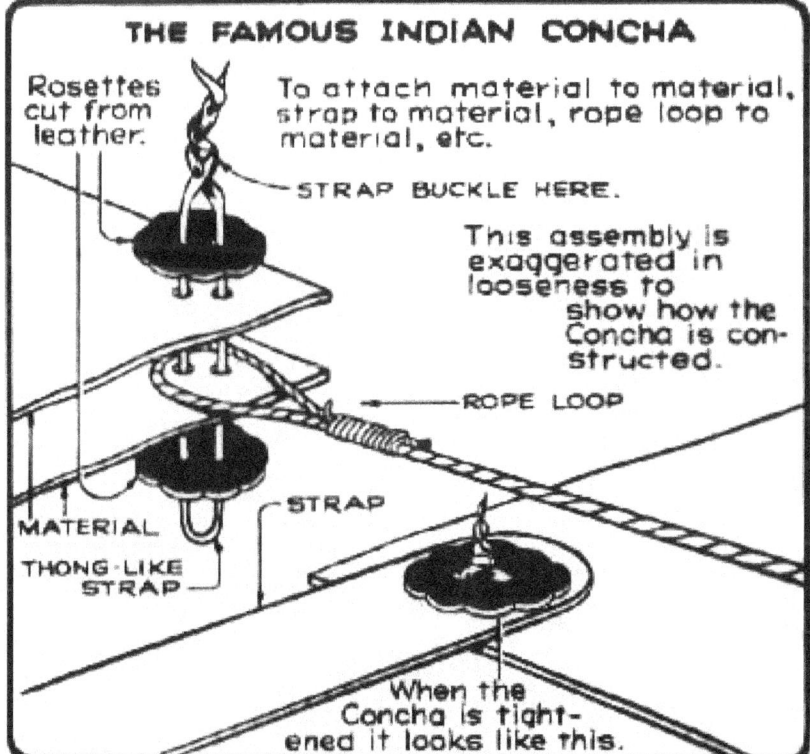

Rosettes cut from leather.

To attach material to material, strap to material, rope loop to material, etc.

STRAP BUCKLE HERE.

This assembly is exaggerated in looseness to show how the Concha is constructed.

ROPE LOOP

MATERIAL
THONG-LIKE STRAP
STRAP

When the Concha is tightened it looks like this.

The Leather Craft shown here will be very useful as a means of construction for many of the items outlined on other Straight Arrow Injun-uity Cards.

For other interesting Leather Craft items See Page No. 40

STRAIGHT ARROW
INDIAN LEATHER CRAFT II

INDIAN STRAP BUCKLE

Strap to strap.
Cut matching holes in each.

Buckle straps together like this. Works well when wet or frozen; when a knot or metal buckle would not work.

INDIAN HITCH BUCKLE

Leather strap to pole, pony to cart etc.

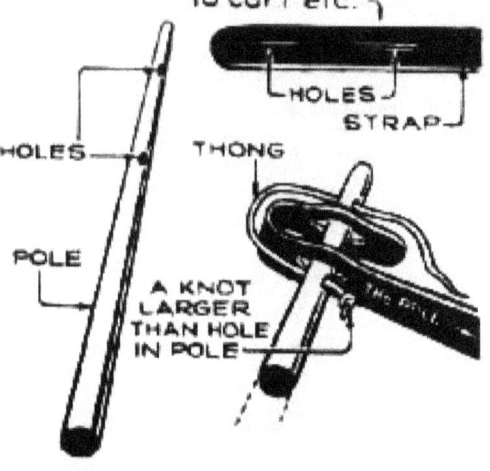

HOLES
STRAP
POLE
THONG
A KNOT LARGER THAN HOLE IN POLE

Assemble like this... You can unhitch this assembly quickly by pulling the thong out of the outside hole, then slip the strap off the pole.

INDIAN SNUB BUCKLE

FOR FASTENING: This end of leather thong or rope is attached to your tent and is used for securing it tightly to the ground.

For fastening down tents, etc., carve a piece of wood about ¾" thick and 5" long to shape shown. Increase dimensions for heavier work.

FOR LIFTING:
By connecting two snub buckles to an object like this you can make many lifting tasks easier.

LOCKED POSITION
KNOT
HOLES
SLIDING POSITION
TO OBJECT

With this arrangement you can lift to greater heights as this will allow for re-knotting the loose ends to keep them within reach.

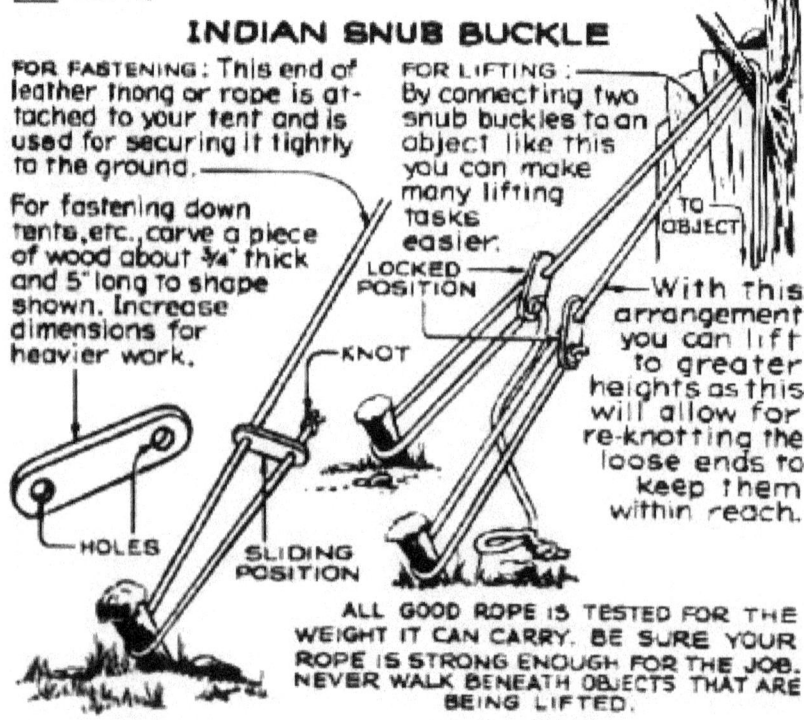

ALL GOOD ROPE IS TESTED FOR THE WEIGHT IT CAN CARRY. BE SURE YOUR ROPE IS STRONG ENOUGH FOR THE JOB. NEVER WALK BENEATH OBJECTS THAT ARE BEING LIFTED.

STRAIGHT ARROW
INDIAN MOCCASINS, PART I

Use soft leather from discarded furniture, shoes or auto upholstery. If not available, use scraps of leatherette or heavy canvas.

MOCCASIN SOLES: Trace the outlines of your feet on two pieces of your material. Add a one-inch border all around. Using scissors, cut out the resultant pattern.

MOCCASIN TOPS Again trace outline of your feet on two other pieces of material. Add allowance as shown. Then with scissors, cut out resultant patterns.

Draw a line like this on the upper side of your two tops to indicate area to be covered by soles.

Join the two ends of the TOP marked "heel," lapping one end an inch over the other. Using strong cord (colored, if possible), sew or lace the two ends together.

Place the TOP upon the SOLE. Turn up the border of the SOLE one inch all around and then sew or lace this turned-up area to the TOP like this.

Turn the side-flaps DOWN

TONGUES Cut out 2 pieces to these dimensions.

Lap the TONGUE one-half inch under the instep and sew on, like this.

Cut fringe on the side-flaps like this.

Sew stitches here on both sides to reinforce.

See Page No. 43 for instruction on finishing and decorating your moccasins.

STRAIGHT ARROW

INDIAN MOCCASINS, PART II

Page No. 41 —INDIAN MOCCASINS PART I- gives all preliminary directions for making moccasins. You are now ready for.....

SECURING MOCCASINS TO YOUR FEET
Punch a row of small holes around the base of the side-flaps, like this —

Lace a colorful cord through the holes like this.

Tie the two ends of the cord together and then turn down the tongue and side-flaps like this.

INDIAN CODE FOR MOCCASIN DECORATION

Indians decorated their moccasins as shown below to indicate proficiency in sports or occupation that required agility of the legs or feet. Use semi-thick oil paint to place the designs on your moccasins.

A BUFFALO HOOF-PRINT
An excellent tracker of game.

TOM-TOM
One of the tribe's ablest dancers or best actors

FIGURE OF A RUNNING MAN
Speedy runner and tribe's messenger.

THREE MOUNTAINS
An excellent and authoritative hunter in mountainous areas.

Most members of an Indian tribe tried hard to develop skills so they could mark their moccasins.

② STRAIGHT ARROW

INDIAN SPURS

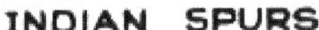

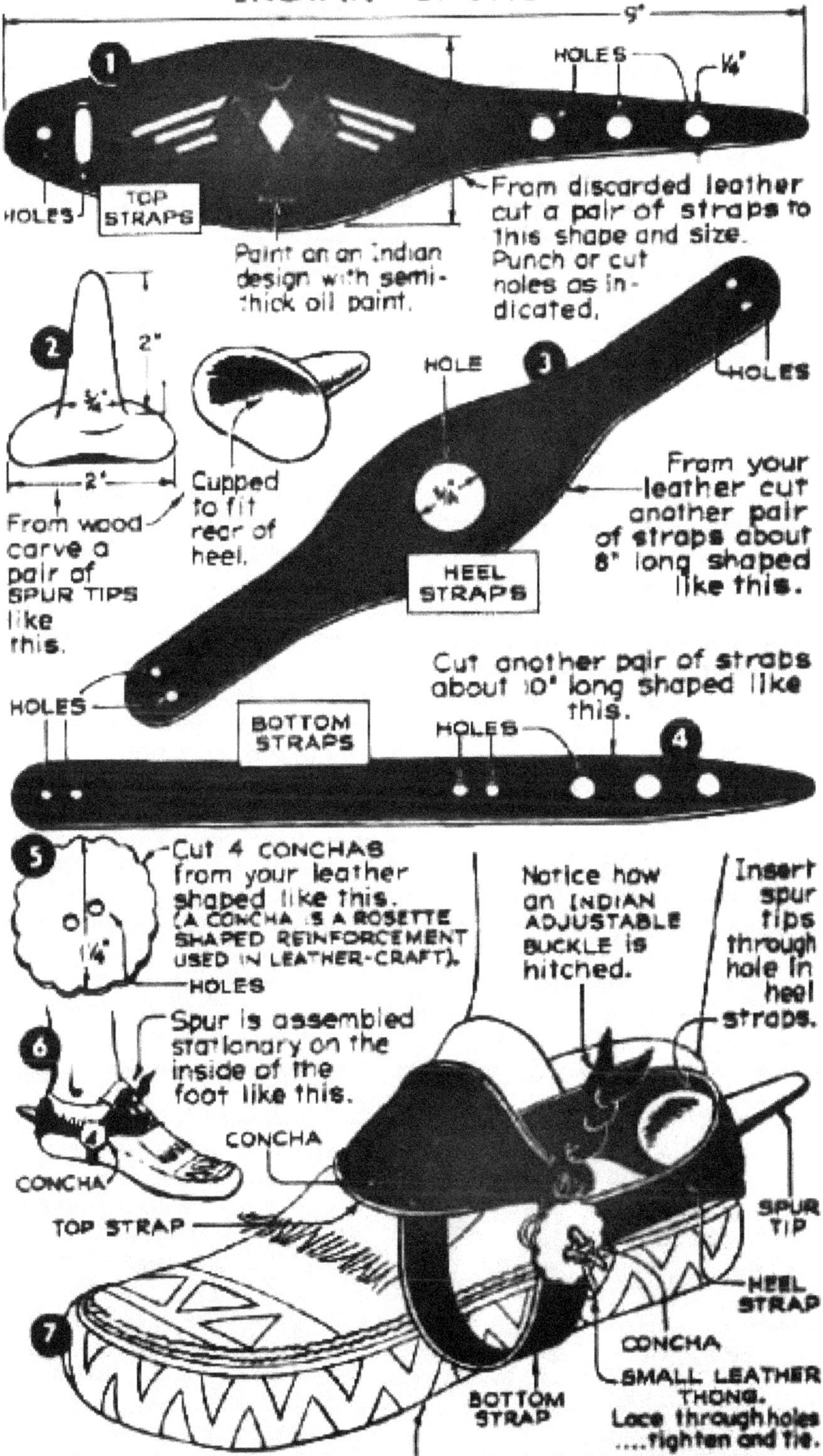

9"
1
HOLES
¼"
HOLES
TOP STRAPS
From discarded leather cut a pair of straps to this shape and size. Punch or cut holes as indicated.
Paint on an Indian design with semi-thick oil paint.
2
2"
¾"
2"
From wood carve a pair of SPUR TIPS like this.
Cupped to fit rear of heel.
HOLE
3
HOLES
¾"
From your leather cut another pair of straps about 8" long shaped like this.
HEEL STRAPS
HOLES
Cut another pair of strabs about 10" long shaped like this.
BOTTOM STRAPS
HOLES
4
5
Cut 4 CONCHAS from your leather shaped like this. (A CONCHA IS A ROSETTE SHAPED REINFORCEMENT USED IN LEATHER-CRAFT).
1¼"
HOLES
Notice how an INDIAN ADJUSTABLE BUCKLE is hitched.
Insert spur tips through hole in heel straps.
6
Spur is assembled stationary on the inside of the foot like this.
CONCHA
CONCHA
TOP STRAP
SPUR TIP
HEEL STRAP
7
CONCHA
SMALL LEATHER THONG. Lace through holes ....tighten and tie.
BOTTOM STRAP

Assemble your spurs like this. It may be necessary to take up the heel and bottom straps to fit your foot. Do this by cutting another set of holes which permit straps to fit you.

STRAIGHT ARROW

INDIAN ARMLETS

Select soft leather from discarded shoes, upholstery, leatherette or heavy canvas.

Cut two pieces of material in this shape and to these specified dimensions.

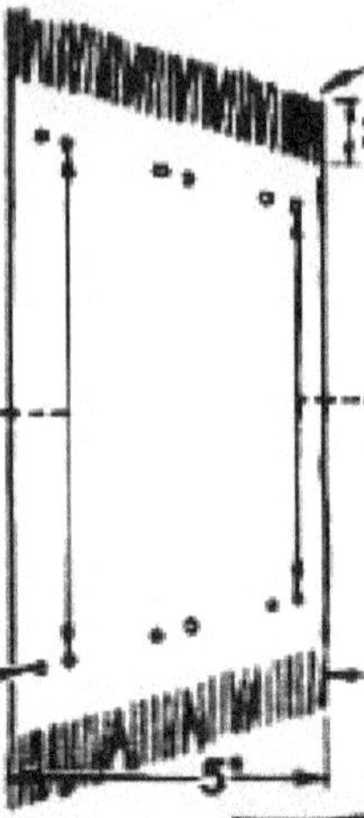

With scissors cut a 2-inch fringe on this edge. 12"

This should be ¾ inch larger than measurement around the forearm.

This should be ¾ inch larger than the measurement around your wrist.

With an ice pick or similar tool, punch 12 holes like this.

With scissors cut a 2-inch fringe on this edge.

5"

Cut six rosettes like this from your material. HOLES 1½"

From your material cut six thongs ³⁄₁₆ inch wide and 8 inches long. Adjust to your arms.

Assemble the parts like this.

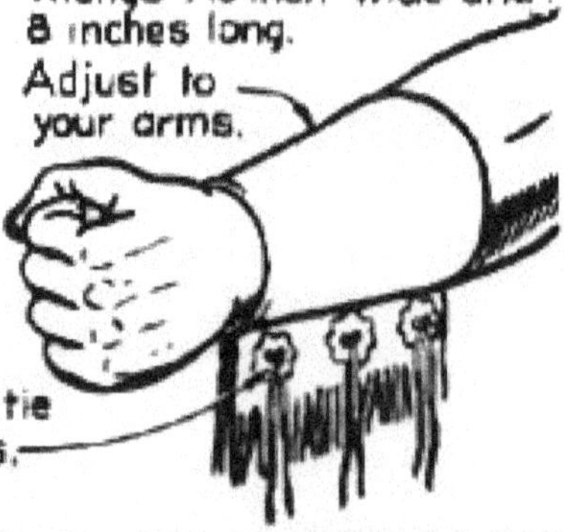

Pull the thongs through the rosettes and tie simple knots.

Use semi-thick oil paint to decorate your armlets.

INDIAN CODE FOR ARMLET DECORATION

Indians decorated their armlets to show outstanding skills they had mastered with their hands and arms.

ARROW HEADS. A champion marksman.

COOKING KETTLE. One of tribe's best cooks.

HORSE'S HEAD. Expert hands for horsemanship.

GRIZZLY BEAR Strongest warrior.

Most members of an Indian tribe tried hard to become outstanding in some line of endeavor so that they could mark their armlets.

② STRAIGHT ARROW
INDIAN BELT

←— This should be the distance around your waist —→

①

4"
4"
4"

Using old leather, leatherette, canvas or similar material cut out this pattern.

Cut a 4" fringe along this edge.

Cut out rectangles 1" larger in width than the regular belt-loops on your denims to allow your regular belt to pass through inside of this Indian Belt and through loops of your denims as well.

DENIM BELT LOOP   CUT-OUT.....RECTANGLES

12"

With semi-thick oil-paint, paint a colorful Indian design on the center section.

Space the rectangles as the belt loops of your denims are spaced.

③

DENIM BELT LOOPS

Fold back the top of top section and sew it to bottom of middle section with strong cord along this line.

YOUR REGULAR BELT

④

Notice how your regular belt comes out through the rectangles to pass through the belt loops of your denims..... Therefore your Indian Belt is practical as well as decorative

J. Meagher

② STRAIGHT ARROW
INDIAN CHAPS (OUT OF DENIMS)

To give your chaps usual Indian form-fit appearance pin a row of pins down outside of pant-legs like this —

Allow play for stocking feet to pass through.→

Remove pants and replace row of pins with a sewed seam.

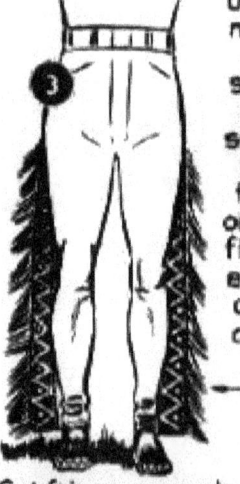

Using leatherette, canvas or similar material cut a chap-flap for each leg to this size and shape in relation to size of your denims.

Using semi-thick oil paint, paint an Indian design on the face of the chap flaps.

Cut fringe along this edge

Using a needle and strong cord sew the chap flaps onto the flattened part of the denims like ←this.

Cut fringe on each end.

Pass the Indian→ Clout between your crotch and inside your belt, front and back like this.

See page No. 45 for instructions to make an attractive Indian Belt.

Using canvas or a similar material cut an INDIAN CLOUT to these dimensions.

Paint an Indian design on each end like this.

40 TO 50 INCHES
4"
7"
4"

The ends of the Indian Clout are allowed to drape straight down the front and back like this.

See page No. 41 for instructions to make your own Indian Moccasins →

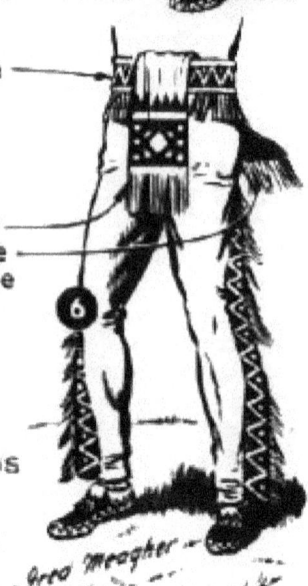

Greg Meagher

STRAIGHT ARROW
COMANCHE WAR BONNET

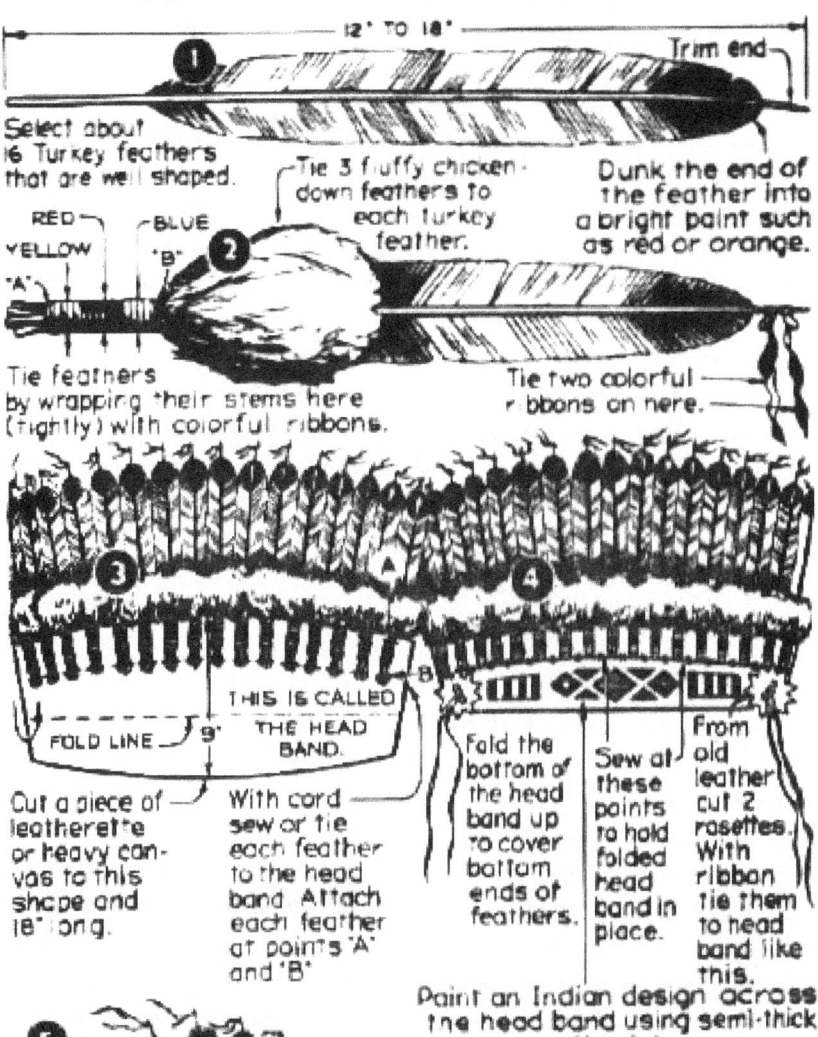

1. Select about 16 Turkey feathers that are well shaped. 12" to 18". Trim end. Dunk the end of the feather into a bright paint such as red or orange.

2. Tie 3 fluffy chicken-down feathers to each turkey feather. Tie feathers by wrapping their stems here (tightly) with colorful ribbons. RED, YELLOW "A", BLUE "B". Tie two colorful ribbons on here.

3. Cut a piece of leatherette or heavy canvas to this shape and 18" long. FOLD LINE, 9", THIS IS CALLED THE HEAD BAND. With cord sew or tie each feather to the head band. Attach each feather at points 'A' and 'B'.

4. Fold the bottom of the head band up to cover bottom ends of feathers. Sew at these points to hold folded head band in place. From old leather cut 2 rosettes. With ribbon tie them to head band like this. Paint an Indian design across the head band using semi-thick oil paint.

5. From a point just in front of each ear hang a pair of squirrel tails, bright ribbons etc.

6. Tie the ribbons which were tied through the rosettes to each other, like this, in back of your head to fit war bonnet to your head size.

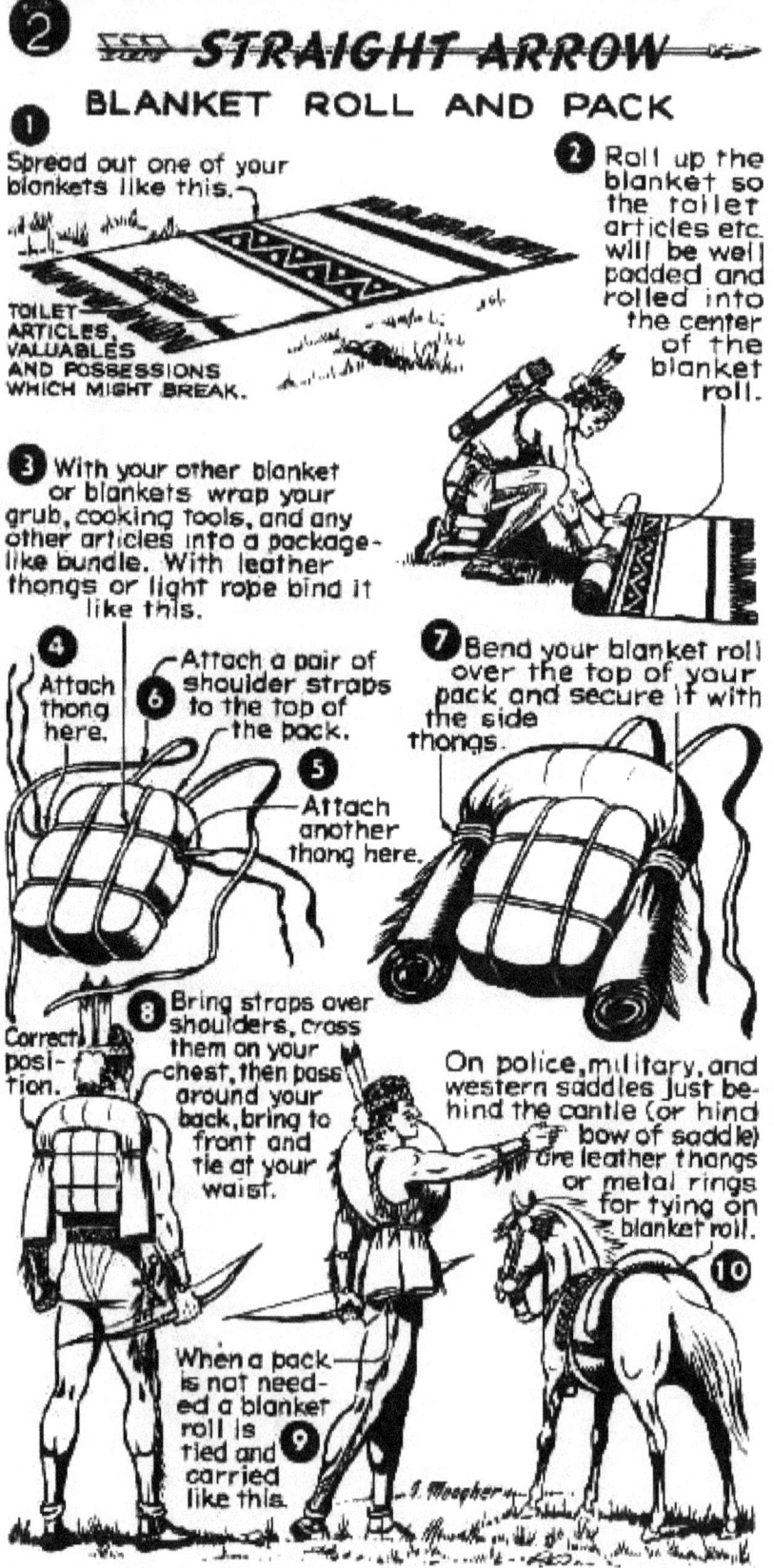

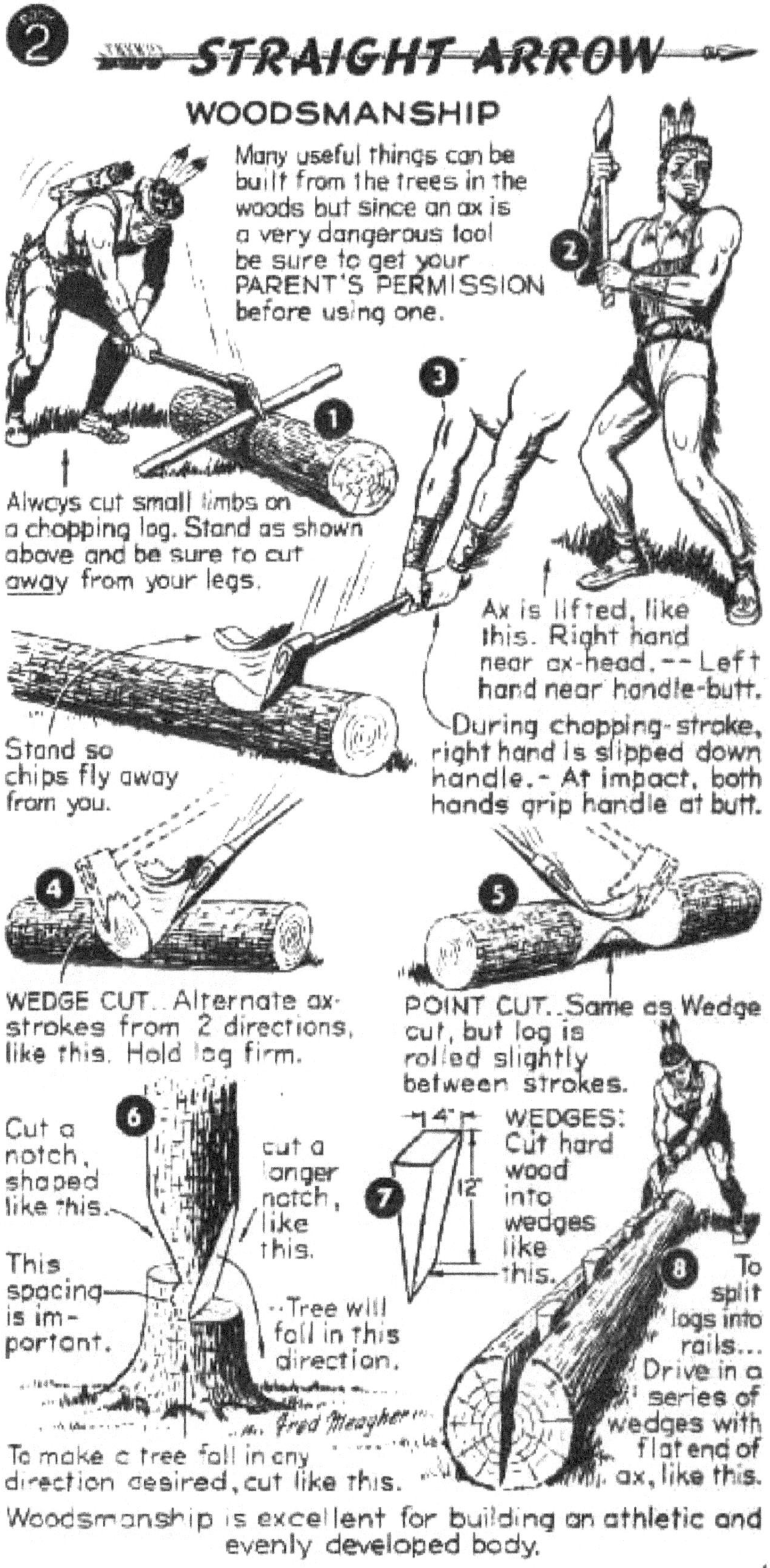

STRAIGHT ARROW

WOODSMANSHIP

Many useful things can be built from the trees in the woods but since an ax is a very dangerous tool be sure to get your PARENT'S PERMISSION before using one.

1. Always cut small limbs on a chopping log. Stand as shown above and be sure to cut *away* from your legs.

2. Ax is lifted, like this. Right hand near ax-head. — Left hand near handle-butt.

3. During chopping-stroke, right hand is slipped down handle. — At impact, both hands grip handle at butt.

Stand so chips fly away from you.

4. WEDGE CUT.. Alternate ax-strokes from 2 directions, like this. Hold log firm.

5. POINT CUT.. Same as Wedge cut, but log is rolled slightly between strokes.

6. Cut a notch, shaped like this. — cut a longer notch, like this.

This spacing is important.

..Tree will fall in this direction.

To make a tree fall in any direction desired, cut like this.

7. WEDGES: Cut hard wood into wedges like this. — 4"— 12"

8. To split logs into rails... Drive in a series of wedges with flat end of ax, like this.

Fred Meagher

Woodsmanship is excellent for building an athletic and evenly developed body.

STRAIGHT ARROW
INDIAN BULL SHIELD

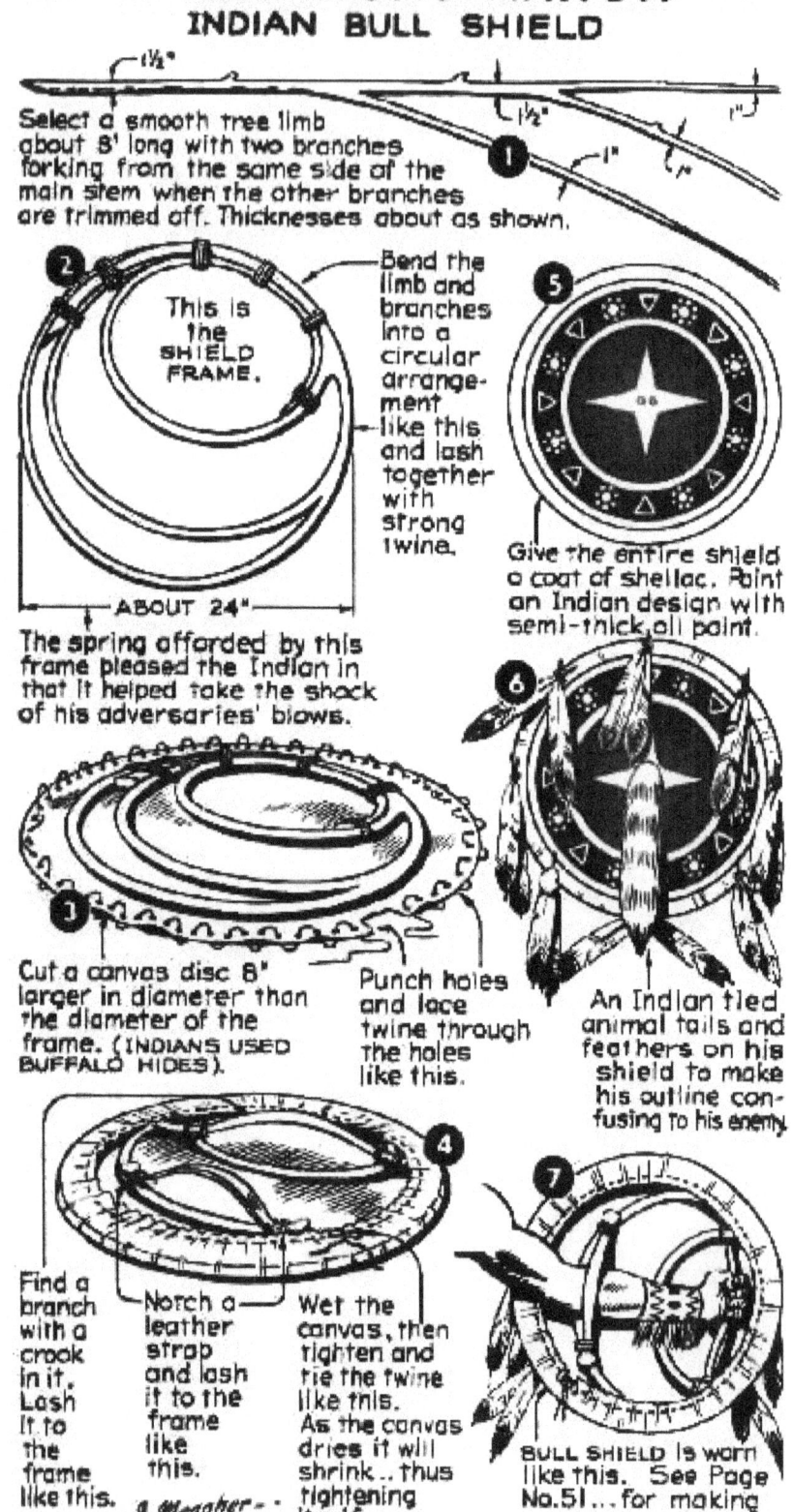

1. Select a smooth tree limb about 8' long with two branches forking from the same side of the main stem when the other branches are trimmed off. Thicknesses about as shown.

2. This is the SHIELD FRAME. Bend the limb and branches into a circular arrangement like this and lash together with strong twine. ABOUT 24"

The spring afforded by this frame pleased the Indian in that it helped take the shock of his adversaries' blows.

3. Cut a canvas disc 8" larger in diameter than the diameter of the frame. (INDIANS USED BUFFALO HIDES). Punch holes and lace twine through the holes like this.

4. Find a branch with a crook in it. Lash it to the frame like this. Notch a leather strap and lash it to the frame like this. Wet the canvas, then tighten and tie the twine like this. As the canvas dries it will shrink... thus tightening itself.

—J. Meagher

5. Give the entire shield a coat of shellac. Paint on Indian design with semi-thick oil paint.

6. An Indian tied animal tails and feathers on his shield to make his outline confusing to his enemy.

7. BULL SHIELD is worn like this. See Page No. 51... for making an INDIAN LANCE.

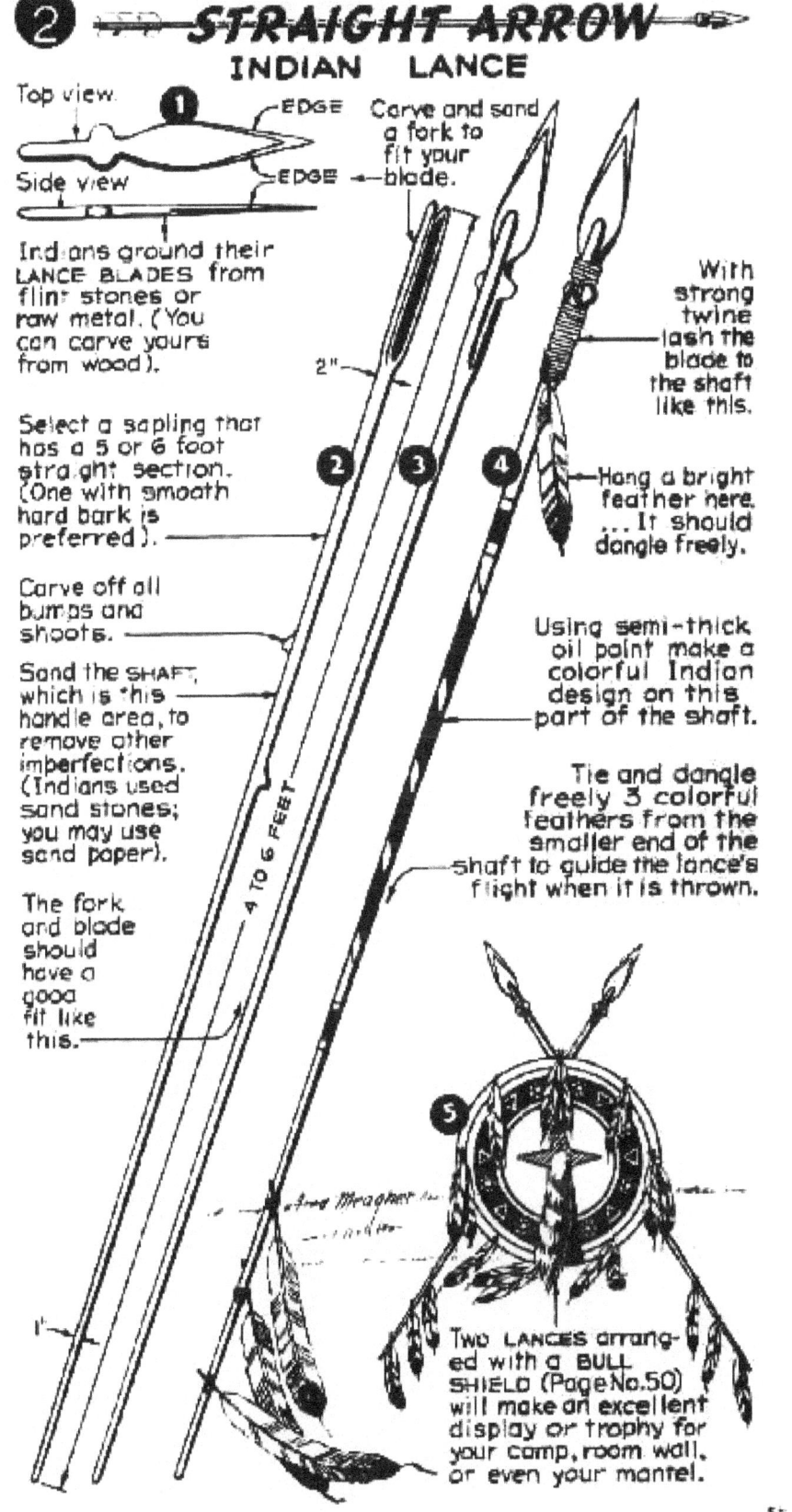

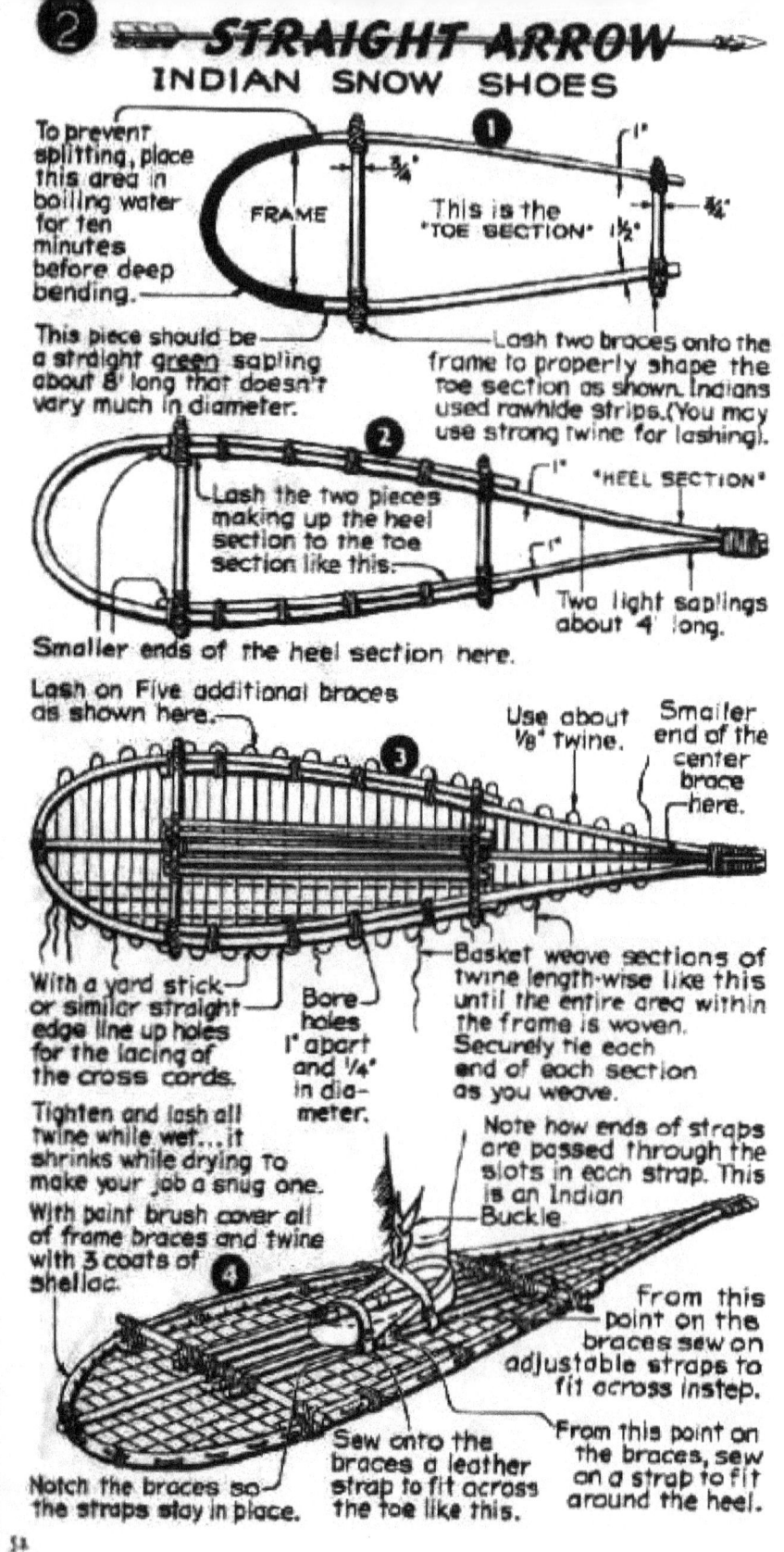

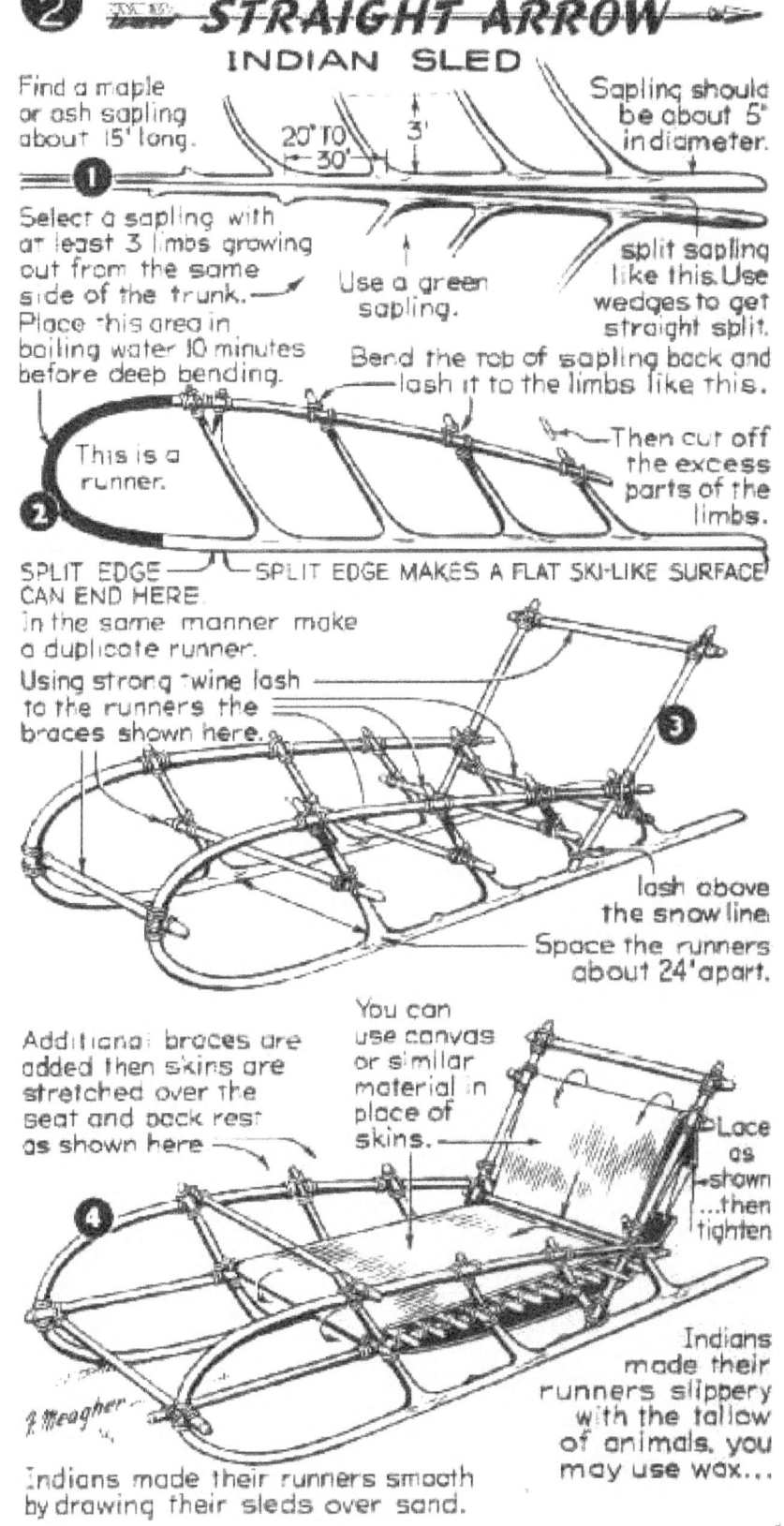

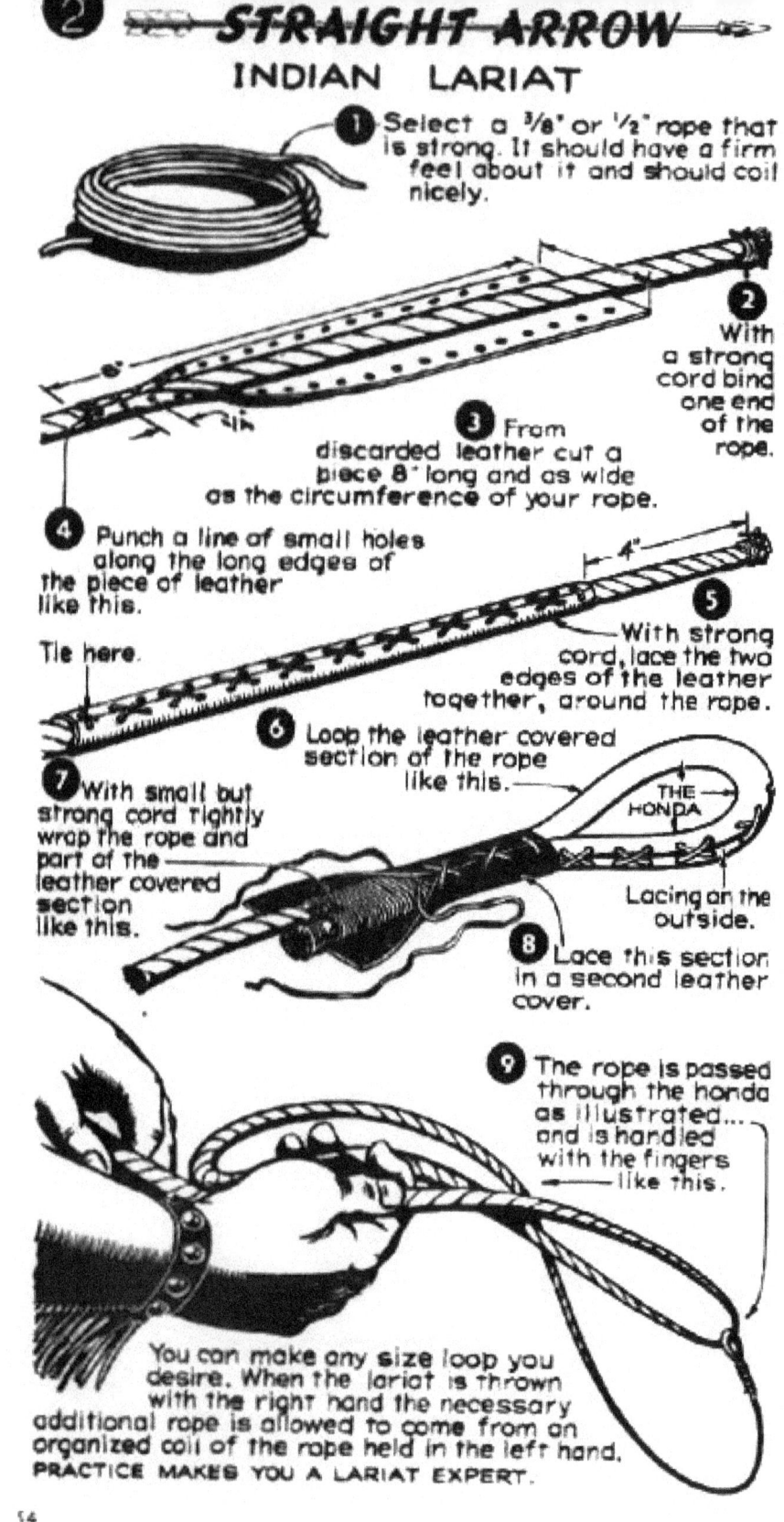

STRAIGHT ARROW
INDIAN HAMMOCK

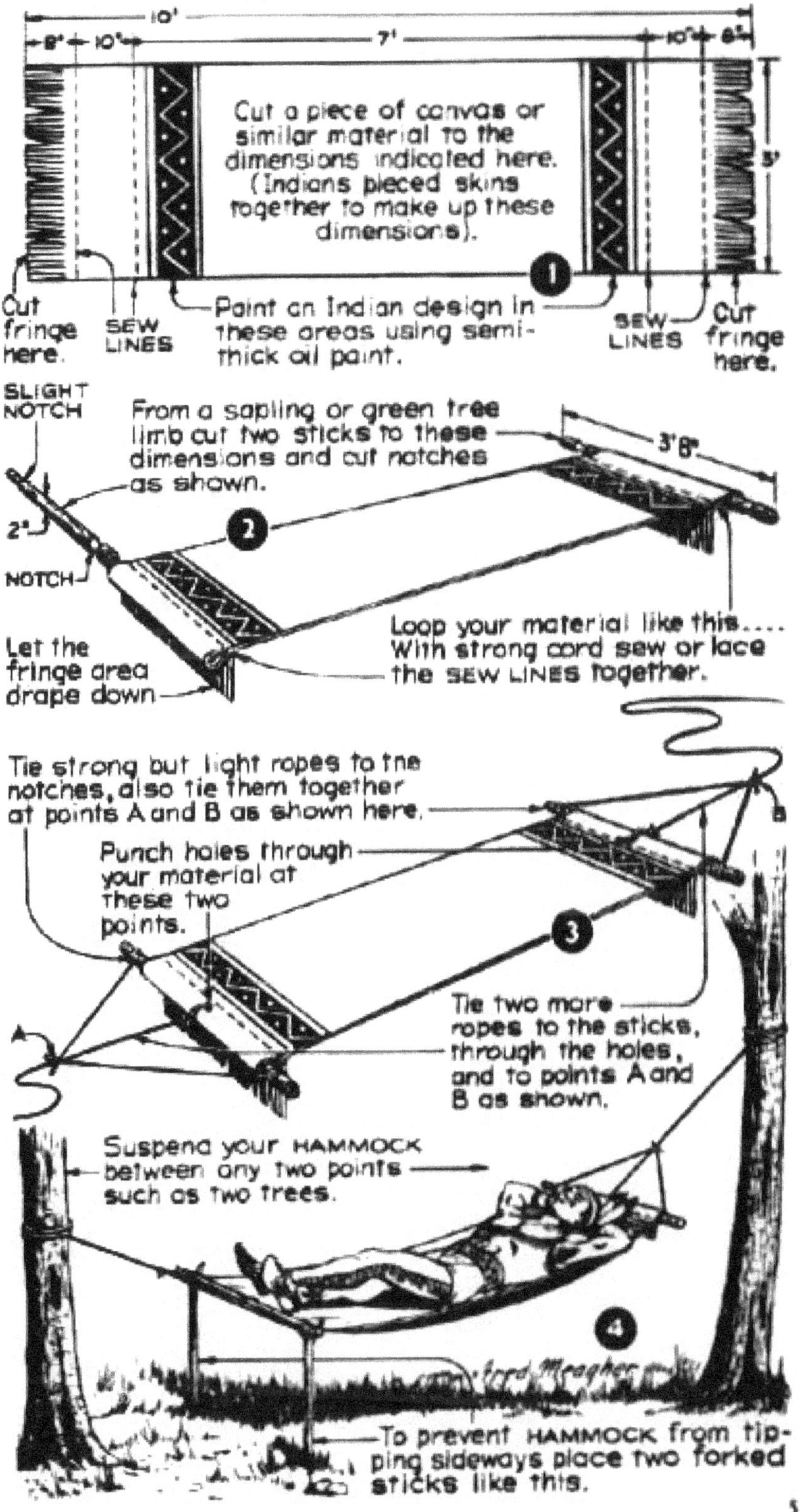

1 Cut a piece of canvas or similar material to the dimensions indicated here. (Indians pieced skins together to make up these dimensions).

Dimensions: 10' overall, with 8" + 10" fringe/sew areas on each side, 7' center; 3' height.

Cut fringe here. SEW LINES — Paint an Indian design in these areas using semi-thick oil paint. — SEW LINES Cut fringe here.

2 SLIGHT NOTCH — From a sapling or green tree limb cut two sticks to these dimensions and cut notches as shown. 3'8"

2" NOTCH

Let the fringe area drape down.

Loop your material like this.... With strong cord sew or lace the SEW LINES together.

3 Tie strong but light ropes to the notches, also tie them together at points A and B as shown here.

Punch holes through your material at these two points.

Tie two more ropes to the sticks, through the holes, and to points A and B as shown.

4 Suspend your HAMMOCK between any two points such as two trees.

To prevent HAMMOCK from tipping sideways place two forked sticks like this.

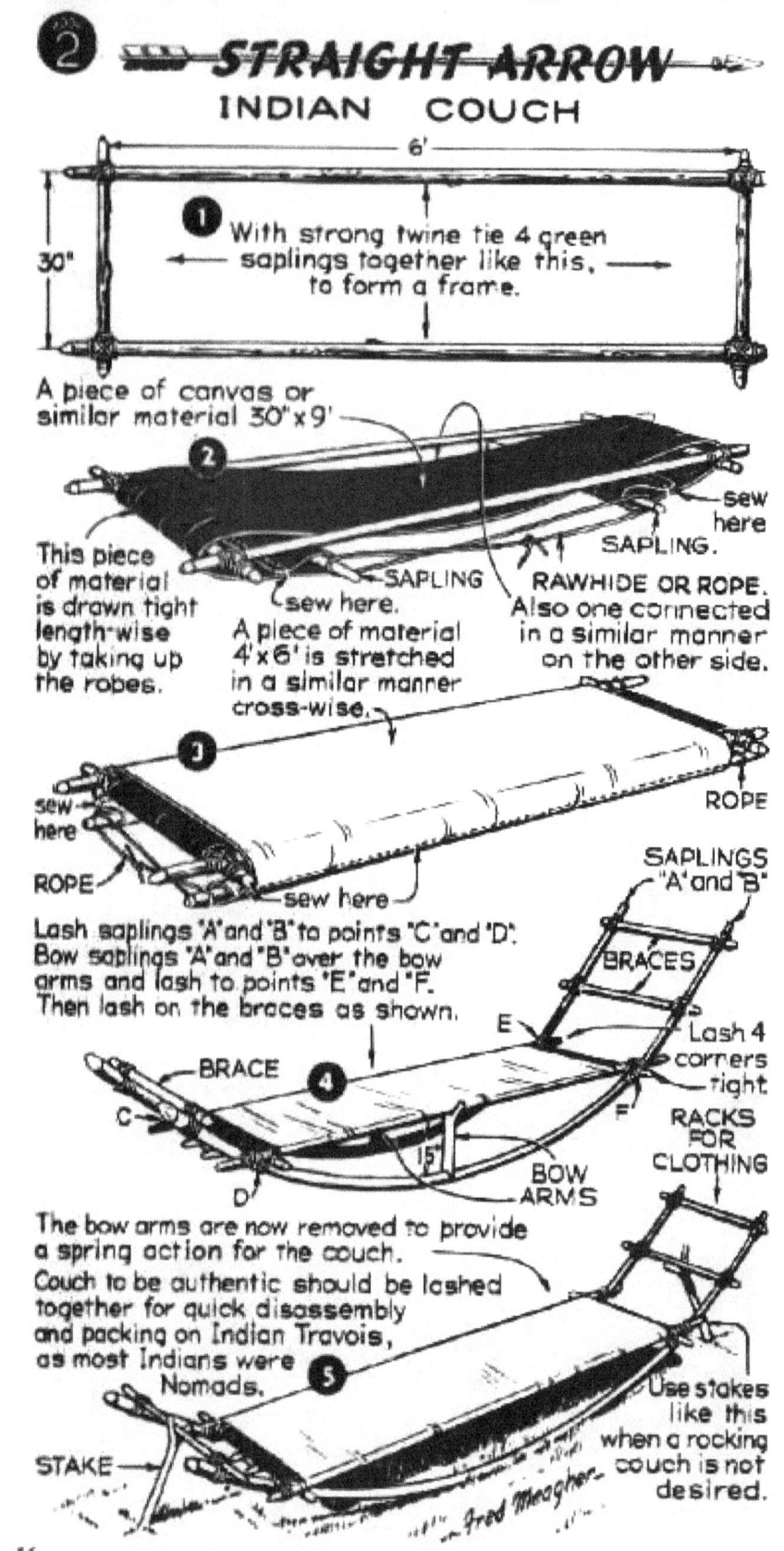

② STRAIGHT ARROW
POW-WOW LODGE or CANOE SHELTER

Indians loved to Pow-wow. They also took great care of their colorful and decorative birch or doeskin canoes; therefore, they usually built a similar shelter for both purposes.

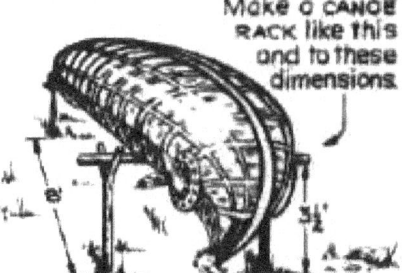
Make a CANOE RACK like this and to these dimensions.

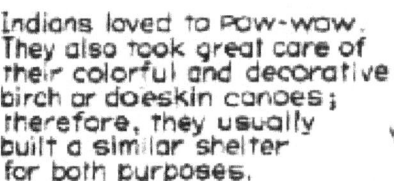

① Cut 10 light saplings 14' long. Dig holes 2' deep and sink the saplings into the holes. The holes should be arranged in this manner.

② Pull the tops of the opposite saplings together and lash them with light strong rope.

③ Lash a pole to the tops of the five arches formed by the ten saplings.

④ Cut off the excess

This is called the "SHELTER FRAME".

Make a cover for your shelter frame by sewing or lacing together sections of burlap, canvas or similar material.

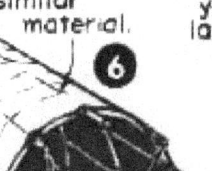

⑥ Bottom pole passes through a sewed hem.

⑤ Lash 8 additional poles to the arches in these positions.

If burlap or canvas is not available you can build a brush shelter by lashing thick brush to your frame.

⑦ Then pile on enough additional brush to keep the hot sun and weather out.

You can increase dimensions if your meeting lodge is to house pow-wows of more than 10 persons.

STRAIGHT ARROW

INDIAN GATES

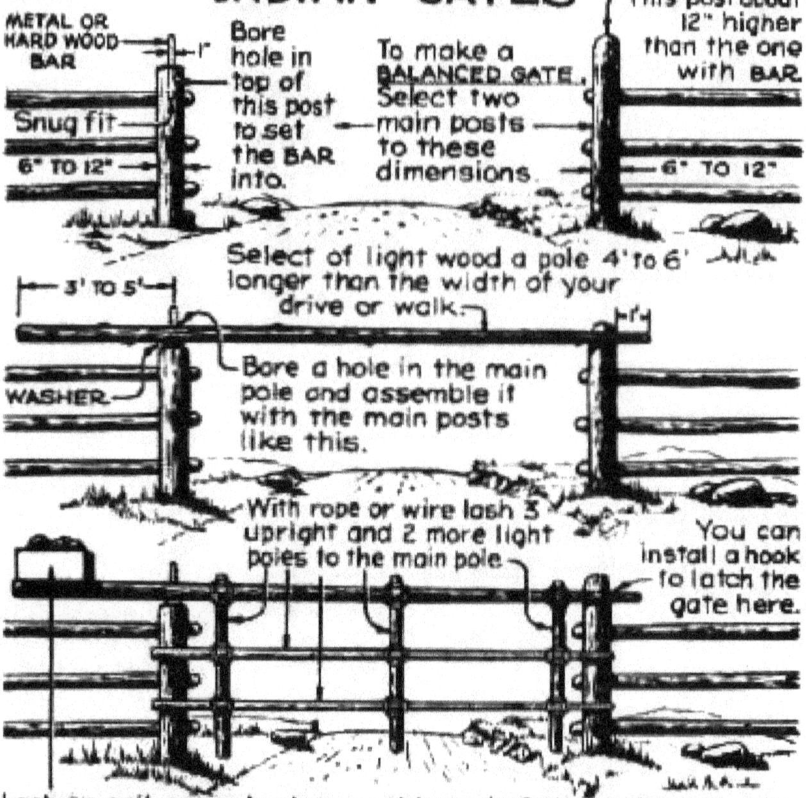

METAL OR HARD WOOD BAR — 1"
Bore hole in top of this post to set the BAR into.
To make a BALANCED GATE. Select two main posts to these dimensions.
This post about 12" higher than the one with BAR.
Snug fit
6" TO 12"
6" TO 12"

3' TO 5'
Select of light wood a pole 4' to 6' longer than the width of your drive or walk.
Bore a hole in the main pole and assemble it with the main posts like this.
WASHER

With rope or wire lash 3 upright and 2 more light poles to the main pole
You can install a hook to latch the gate here.

Lash or nail a wooden box on this end of the main pole. Pile stones into the box until the gate is in perfect balance. — You should be able to open and close this gate with one finger.

MAN GATE

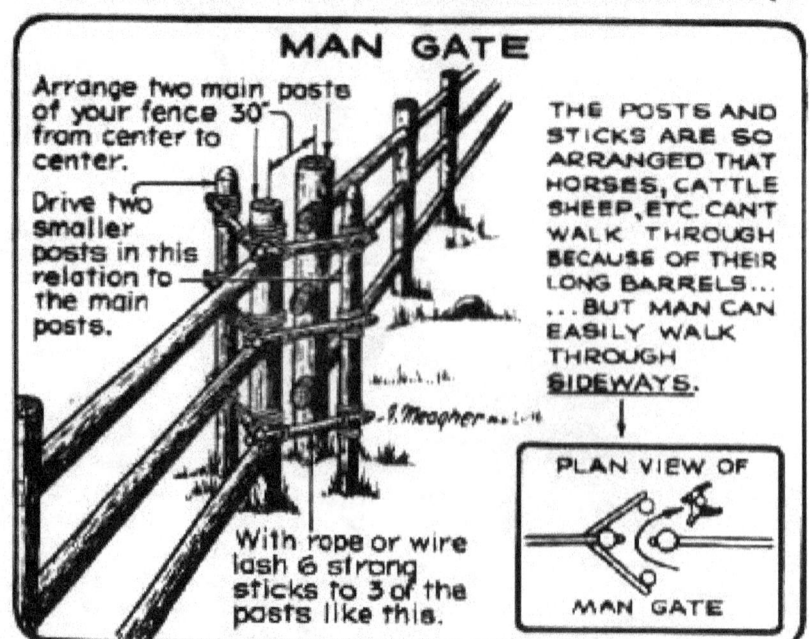

Arrange two main posts of your fence 30" from center to center.

Drive two smaller posts in this relation to the main posts.

THE POSTS AND STICKS ARE SO ARRANGED THAT HORSES, CATTLE SHEEP, ETC. CAN'T WALK THROUGH BECAUSE OF THEIR LONG BARRELS...
...BUT MAN CAN EASILY WALK THROUGH SIDEWAYS.

PLAN VIEW OF MAN GATE

With rope or wire lash 6 strong sticks to 3 of the posts like this.

STRAIGHT ARROW
CANOEMANSHIP

To paddle and steer a canoe on a straight course push paddle slightly away from canoe and drag in water after each stroke....

....until bow comes back on desired course. To paddle silently while stalking game or fish, Indians then turned paddle blade in, parallel to the side of the canoe, so that it could cut through the water to the starting position of a new stroke.

To make a left turn paddle on right side of canoe.

The paddle is shifted from one side to the other for turning or to rest tired arms.

To make a right turn paddle on left side of canoe.

When canoeing with swift current always be sure to keep the prow headed in the general direction the current is flowing. (DON'T LET THE CANOE GET CROSS-CURRENT).

NEVER GO CANOEING UNLESS YOU CAN SWIM.

In case your canoe upsets in deep water don't try to right it!.... But you can swim to one of its ends and it will make a good swimming support, especially if you have a long distance to swim.

39

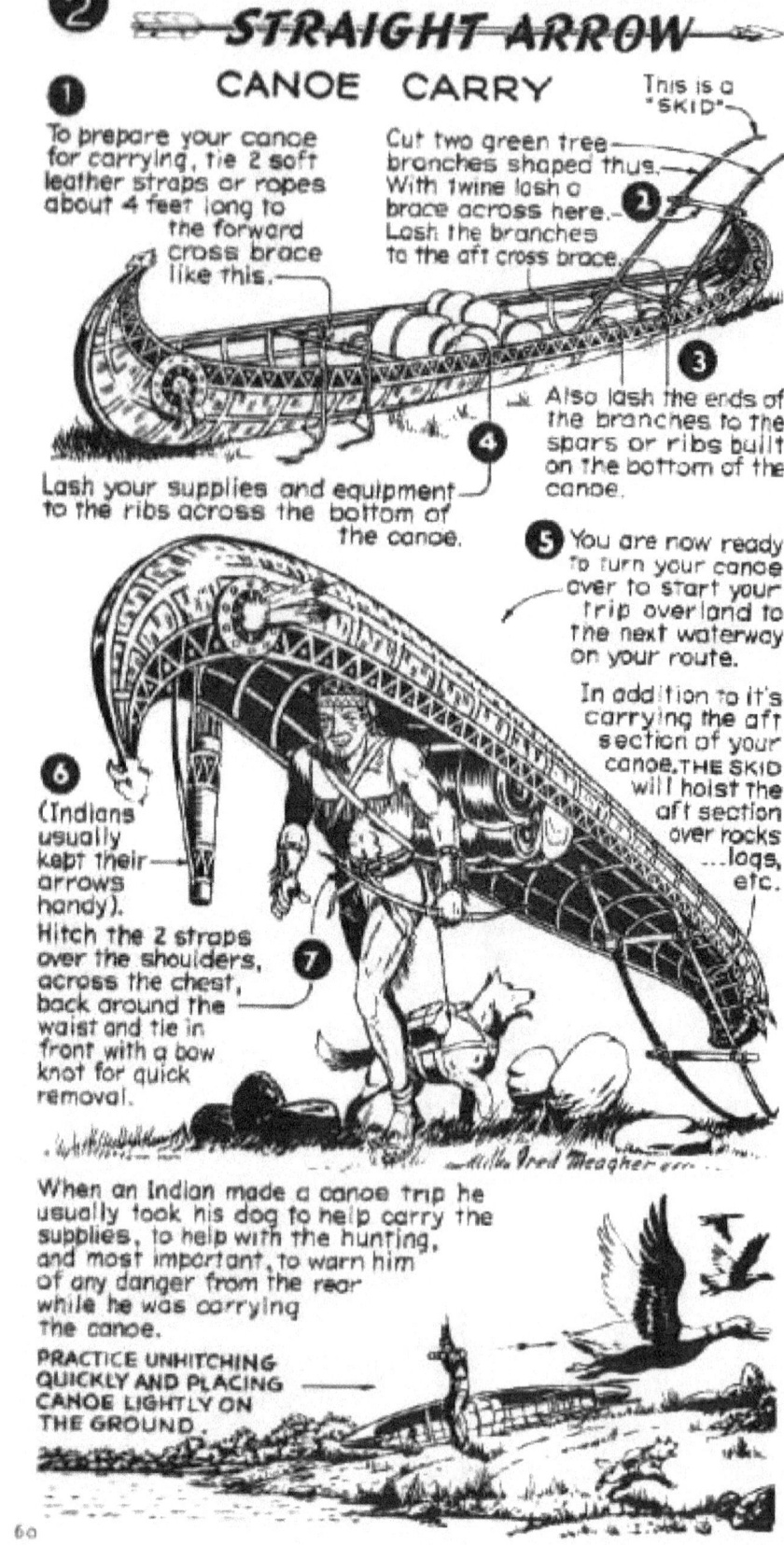

BOOK 2 — STRAIGHT ARROW
INDIAN POTTERY AND UTENSILS

1 — Mix any clay with water until you have a soup-like mixture...

2 — let it set until it dries out to a consistency of pie dough.

3 — With your hands roll the clay out into a number of thin rolls like this. (½", ½", BOARD OR FLAT SURFACE)

4 — Coil one of the rolls to form the base of your container.

5 — Lay coils of the clay layer on layer to the desired shape of your container.

6 — With one hand inside and one out... and directly opposite each other push and rub the coils into a smooth surface.

TAKE YOUR TIME WITH THIS STEP BECAUSE YOU CAN SHAPE YOUR CONTAINER WHERE THE COIL LAYERS ARE UNEVEN.

7 Set your container aside to dry.

8 When it is dry, ask mother if she will place it in her oven when she bakes. Most clays require at least one hour at 500°F. to become "soft-fired". (something like a gardening pot).

9 ..When your container has cooled, cover it with an Indian design using semi-thick oil paint.

If you want your container to be **real** Indian fired, you can build an Indian Kiln... instructions found on Page No. 62.

THESE ARE SOME SUGGESTED SHAPES AND DESIGNS FOR INDIAN POTTERY AND UTENSILS.

STRAIGHT ARROW
INDIAN KILN

1 Place your piece (or pieces) of pottery to be fired on a flat stone. The flat stone should be slightly larger than the widest part of your piece.

2 Arrange four more flat stones in this manner to form four walls around your piece like this.

3 Place a fifth flat stone on top of the four stones forming the sides to form a top like this.

4 Arrange four large logs around the stone enclosure like this. (TO DRIVE THE HEAT AGAINST THE ROCKS).

LEAVE THE CORNERS OPEN FOR A DRAFT

LEAVE AT LEAST ONE FOOT OF SPACE BETWEEN THE STONES AND THE LOGS ON ALL FOUR SIDES.

5 Build a fire in the space between the stones and the logs. Keep building the fire up with wood until the fire partially covers the stones. Keep this fire going for about 6 hours. Keep hot coals moved against the stones, and keep the ashes well removed.

SEE PAGE No. 61 ...FOR INSTRUCTIONS FOR PREPARING AND DECORATING INDIAN POTTERY.

STRAIGHT ARROW WANTS ALL BOYS AND GIRLS TO ASK FOR THEIR PARENT'S PERMISSION BEFORE OPERATING AN INDIAN KILN.

STRAIGHT ARROW
BIRD SHELTER AND WEATHER VANE

By following Straight Arrow's instructions below you can build a safe bird shelter that will soon attract a pair of happy occupants.

Set it out in the Springtime, when mating birds are seeking a shelter for a nest.

Birds instinctively know the habits and treachery of their natural enemies and usually will not occupy a vulnerable shelter.

Don't place on poles or attach to trees as houses could be easily reached by cats or other raiders.

cats, raccoons, rodents and many other animals can climb most any where.

Killer or egg-sucking birds will rob and destroy the homes of smaller birds if they can gain entry.

A STRAIGHT ARROW BIRD SHELTER is always suspended from a tree limb by a strong, slender thong. (you can use wire).

Remove nearby limbs stout enough to support a small animal.

Have ready a smaller door in case small birds move in.

Paint shelter to match the tree.
Place dried grass and hair within.

Place this hole where the home hangs in balance.

3'

12"

All animals of prey are afraid to climb or slide down a wire

Place a rudder here and the bird shelter will also act as a weather vane. The rear will always face into the wind and cold winds won't blow in the front door.

Side view of slide arrangement necessary for the sliding door.

The weather vane can be made more effective by adding a secondary rudder on the bottom.

NOTICE HOW QUICKLY BIRDS WILL RECOGNIZE A HOME.

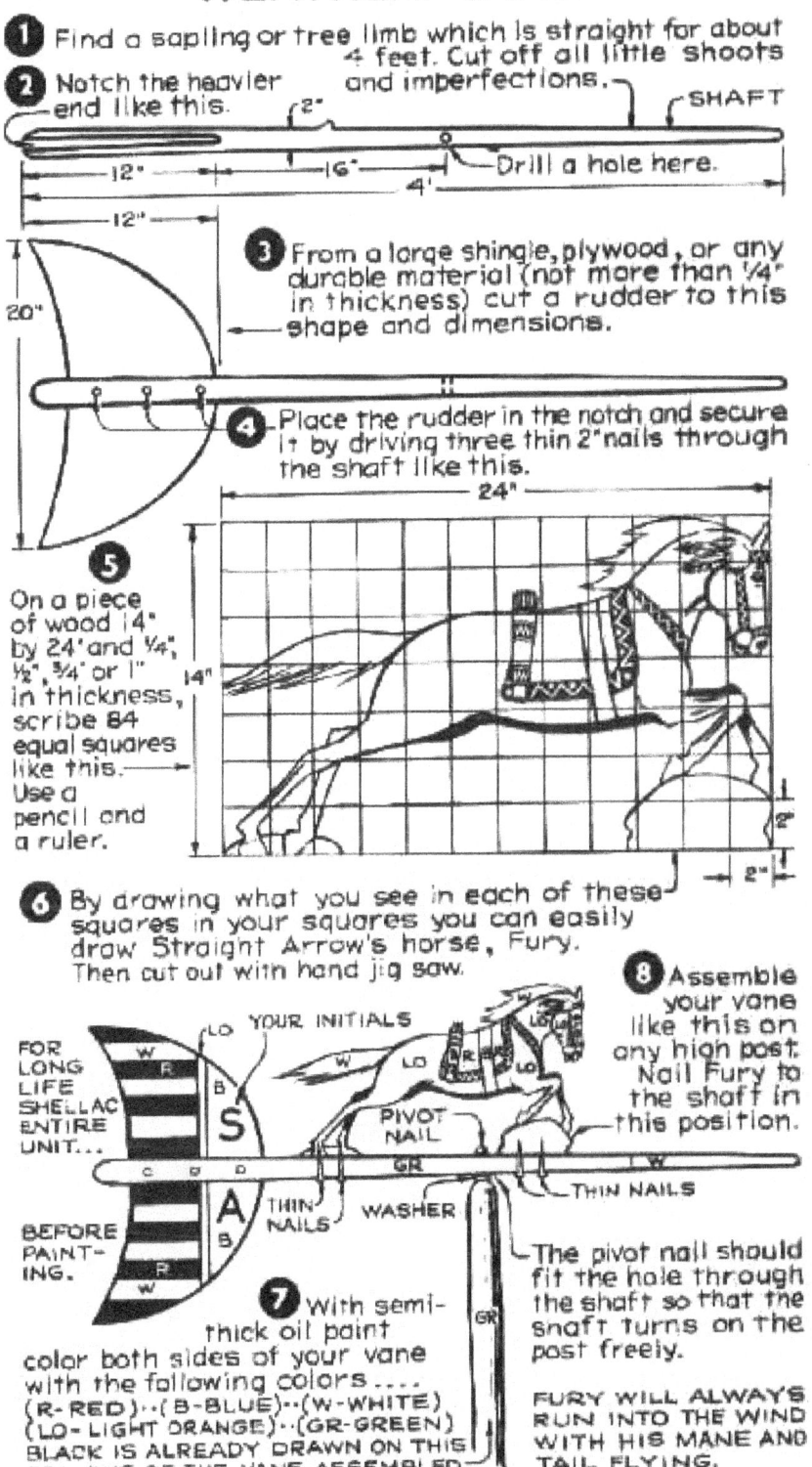

STRAIGHT ARROW
ANIMAL TRAP (PORTABLE)

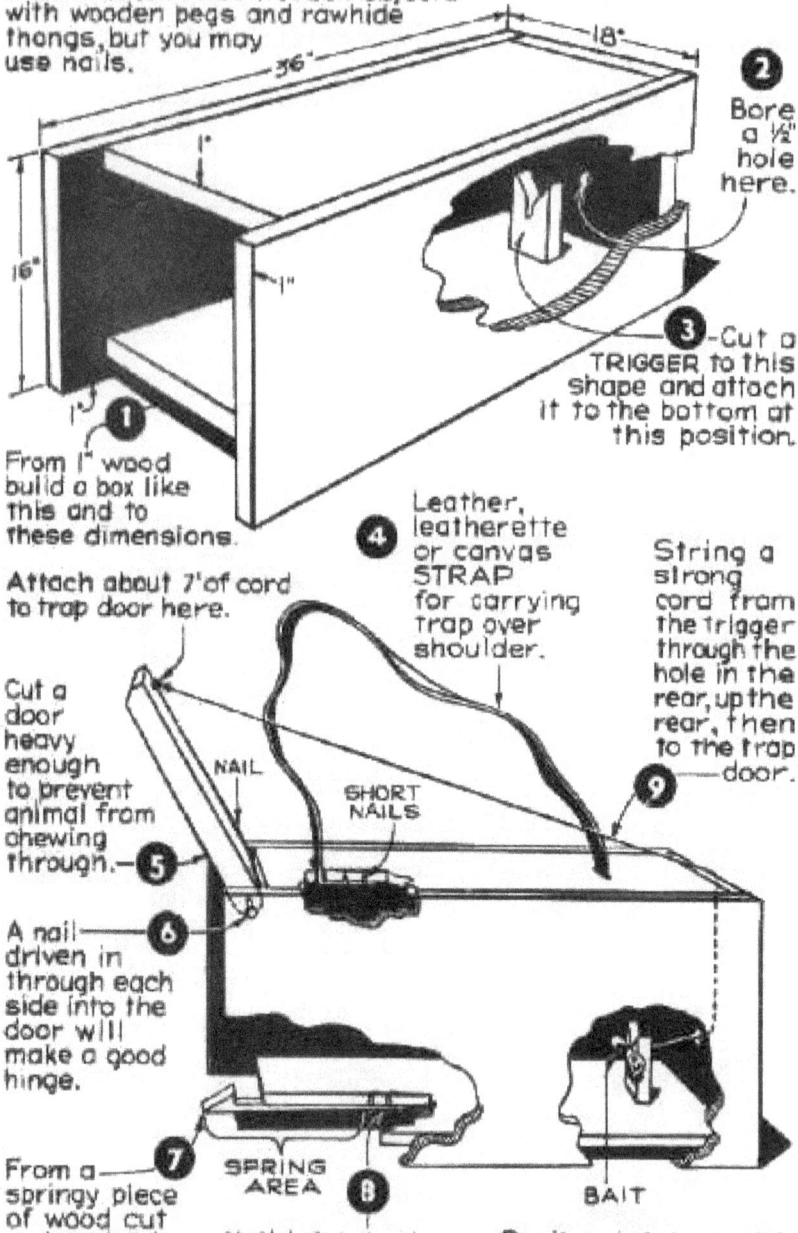

Indians constructed wooden objects with wooden pegs and rawhide thongs, but you may use nails.

① From 1" wood build a box like this and to these dimensions.

② Bore a ½" hole here.

③ Cut a TRIGGER to this shape and attach it to the bottom at this position.

Attach about 7' of cord to trap door here.

④ Leather, leatherette or canvas STRAP for carrying trap over shoulder.

⑨ String a strong cord from the trigger through the hole in the rear, up the rear, then to the trap door.

⑤ Cut a door heavy enough to prevent animal from chewing through.

⑥ A nail driven in through each side into the door will make a good hinge.

⑦ From a springy piece of wood cut a door latch shaped like this.

⑧ Nail latch to the bottom, back at this position.

BAIT

Don't paint trap with bright paint, but finish it to match the surroundings where it is to be used. After an actual setting, sprinkle leaves, dirt, twigs etc. in and around it to give natural appearance.

Trap door, hinge and latch should operate freely, but don't handle them too much before actually setting the trap to catch wild game.

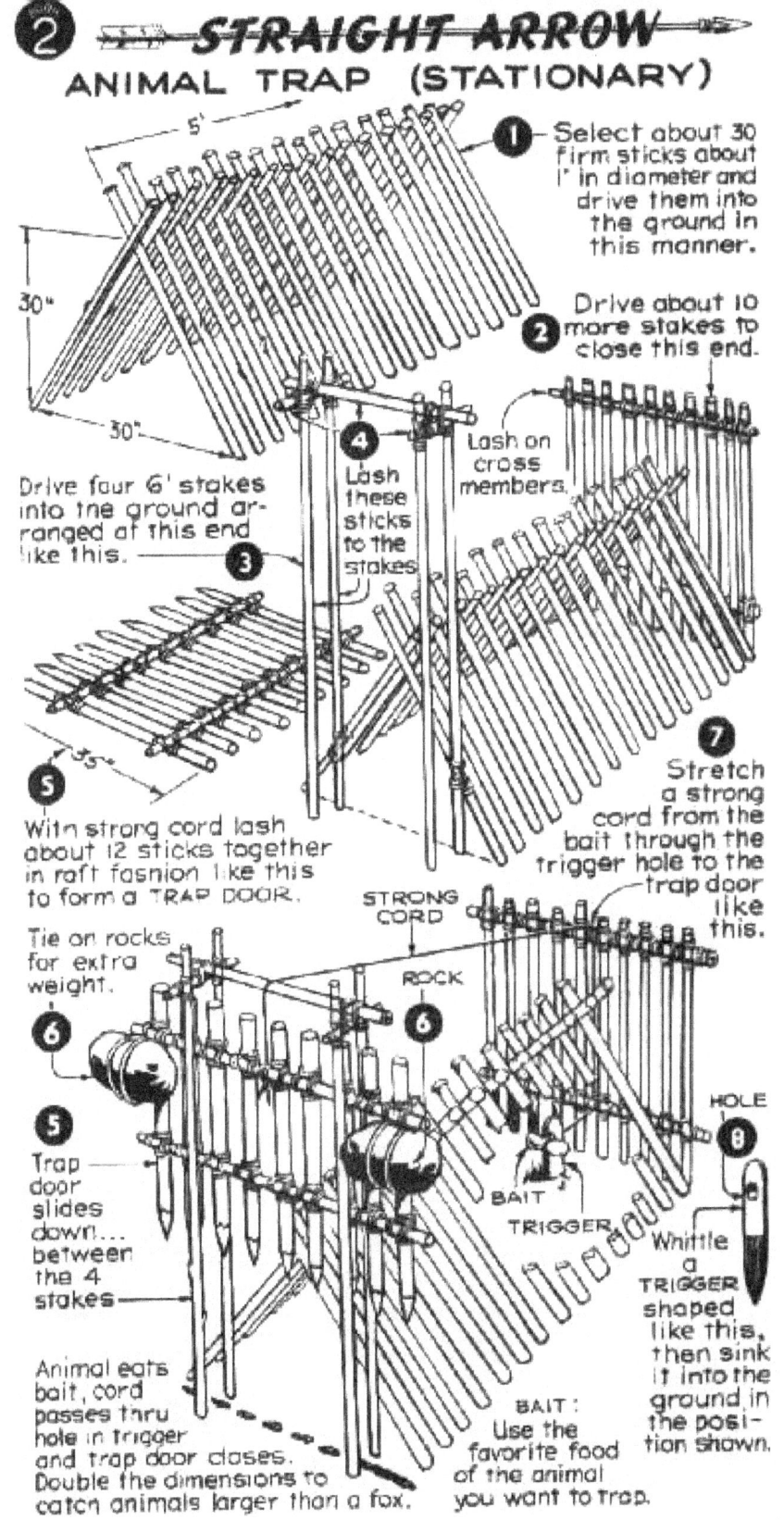

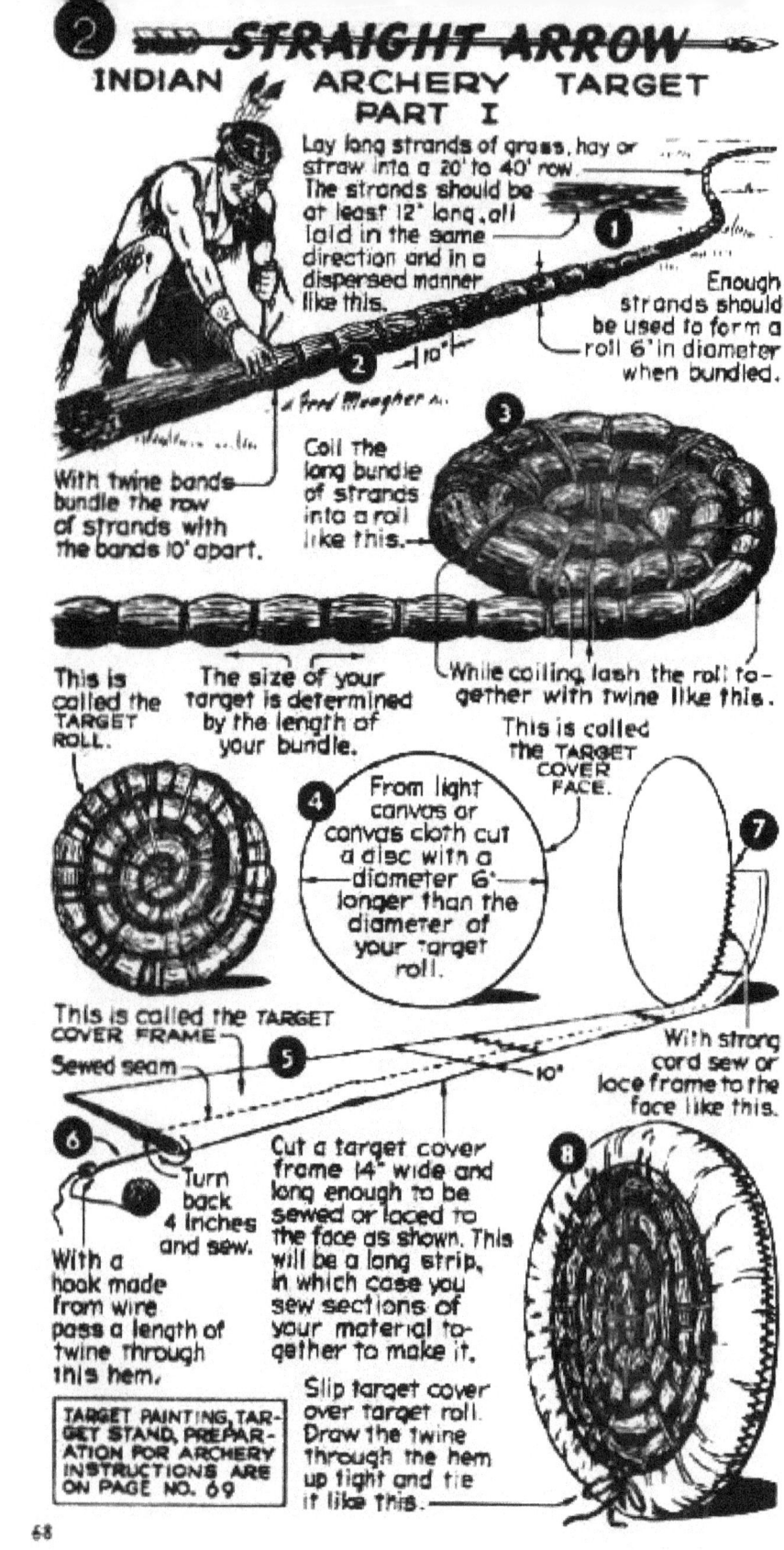

STRAIGHT ARROW
INDIAN ARCHERY TARGET .... PART II

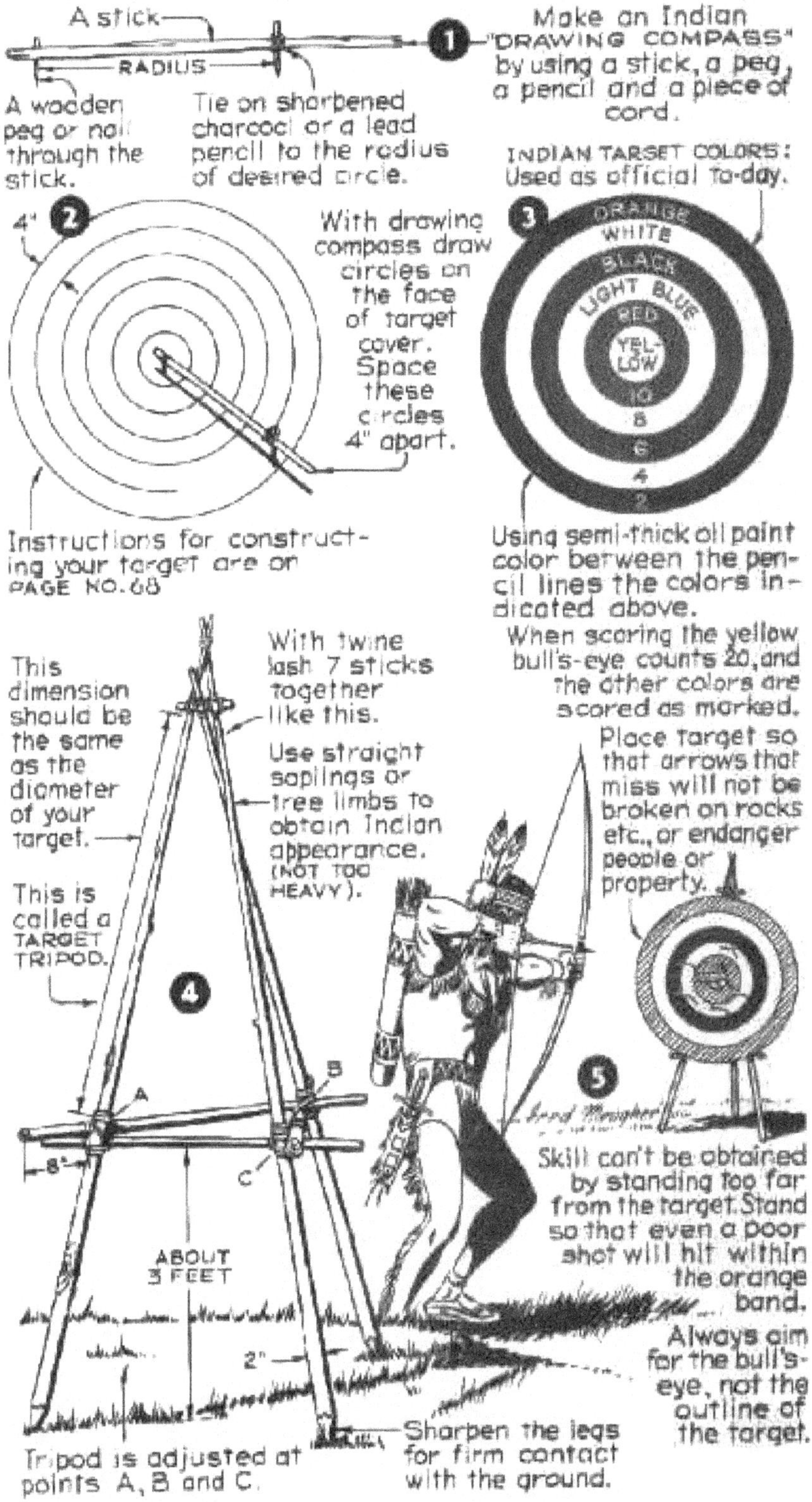

1 Make an Indian "DRAWING COMPASS" by using a stick, a peg, a pencil and a piece of cord.

A stick — RADIUS

A wooden peg or nail through the stick.

Tie on sharpened charcoal or a lead pencil to the radius of desired circle.

2 With drawing compass draw circles on the face of target cover. Space these circles 4" apart.

Instructions for constructing your target are on PAGE NO. 68

3 INDIAN TARGET COLORS: Used as official to-day.

ORANGE
WHITE
BLACK
LIGHT BLUE
RED
YELLOW
10
8
6
4
2

Using semi-thick oil paint color between the pencil lines the colors indicated above.

When scoring the yellow bull's-eye counts 20, and the other colors are scored as marked.

4 This dimension should be the same as the diameter of your target.

This is called a TARGET TRIPOD.

With twine lash 7 sticks together like this.

Use straight saplings or tree limbs to obtain Indian appearance. (NOT TOO HEAVY).

ABOUT 3 FEET

Tripod is adjusted at points A, B and C.

Sharpen the legs for firm contact with the ground.

5 Place target so that arrows that miss will not be broken on rocks etc., or endanger people or property.

Skill can't be obtained by standing too far from the target. Stand so that even a poor shot will hit within the orange band.

Always aim for the bull's-eye, not the outline of the target.

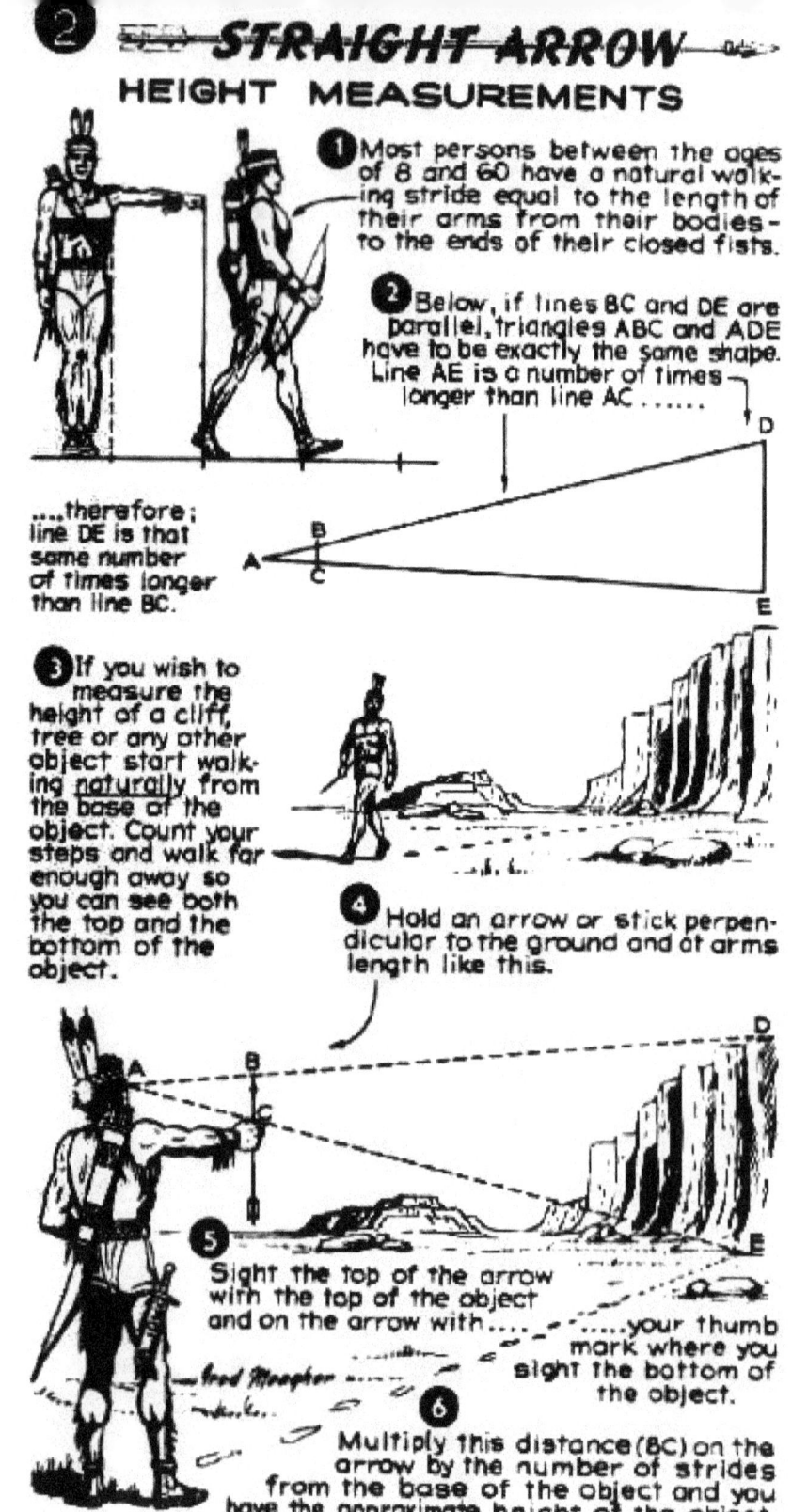

STRAIGHT ARROW
HEIGHT MEASUREMENTS

1 Most persons between the ages of 8 and 60 have a natural walking stride equal to the length of their arms from their bodies - to the ends of their closed fists.

2 Below, if lines BC and DE are parallel, triangles ABC and ADE have to be exactly the same shape. Line AE is a number of times longer than line AC......

....therefore; line DE is that same number of times longer than line BC.

3 If you wish to measure the height of a cliff, tree or any other object start walking _naturally_ from the base of the object. Count your steps and walk far enough away so you can see both the top and the bottom of the object.

4 Hold an arrow or stick perpendicular to the ground and at arms length like this.

5 Sight the top of the arrow with the top of the object and on the arrow with.... .....your thumb mark where you sight the bottom of the object.

6 Multiply this distance (BC) on the arrow by the number of strides from the base of the object and you have the approximate height of the object.

② STRAIGHT ARROW
SUN AND WATCH COMPASS

IF YOU CAN SEE THE SUN AND YOU HAVE A WATCH WITH THE APPROXIMATE TIME: ••• THEN YOU ALSO HAVE A COMPASS.

① Stand with your left shoulder facing in the general direction of the sun.

② Hold your watch flat in the palm of your right hand.

③ Rest one end of a fine twig on the rim of your watch, where the hour hand points to the rim. Twig should be held perpendicular to face of watch.

④ Turn your hand until the shadow of the twig falls along the hour hand as illustrated.

⑤ THE READING OF THE COMPASS

BEFORE NOON:······south will lie halfway between the hour hand and 12...measuring ahead of the hour hand as illustrated. (Local Standard Time only.)

AT NOON: the hour hand will point directly to the south when it is in the shadow of the twig.

IN THE AFTERNOONS: south still lies between the hour hand (in the shadow of the twig) and 12-but you measure back of the hour hand.

THESE INSTRUCTIONS ARE FOR ANY LOCATION **NORTH** OF THE EQUATOR.

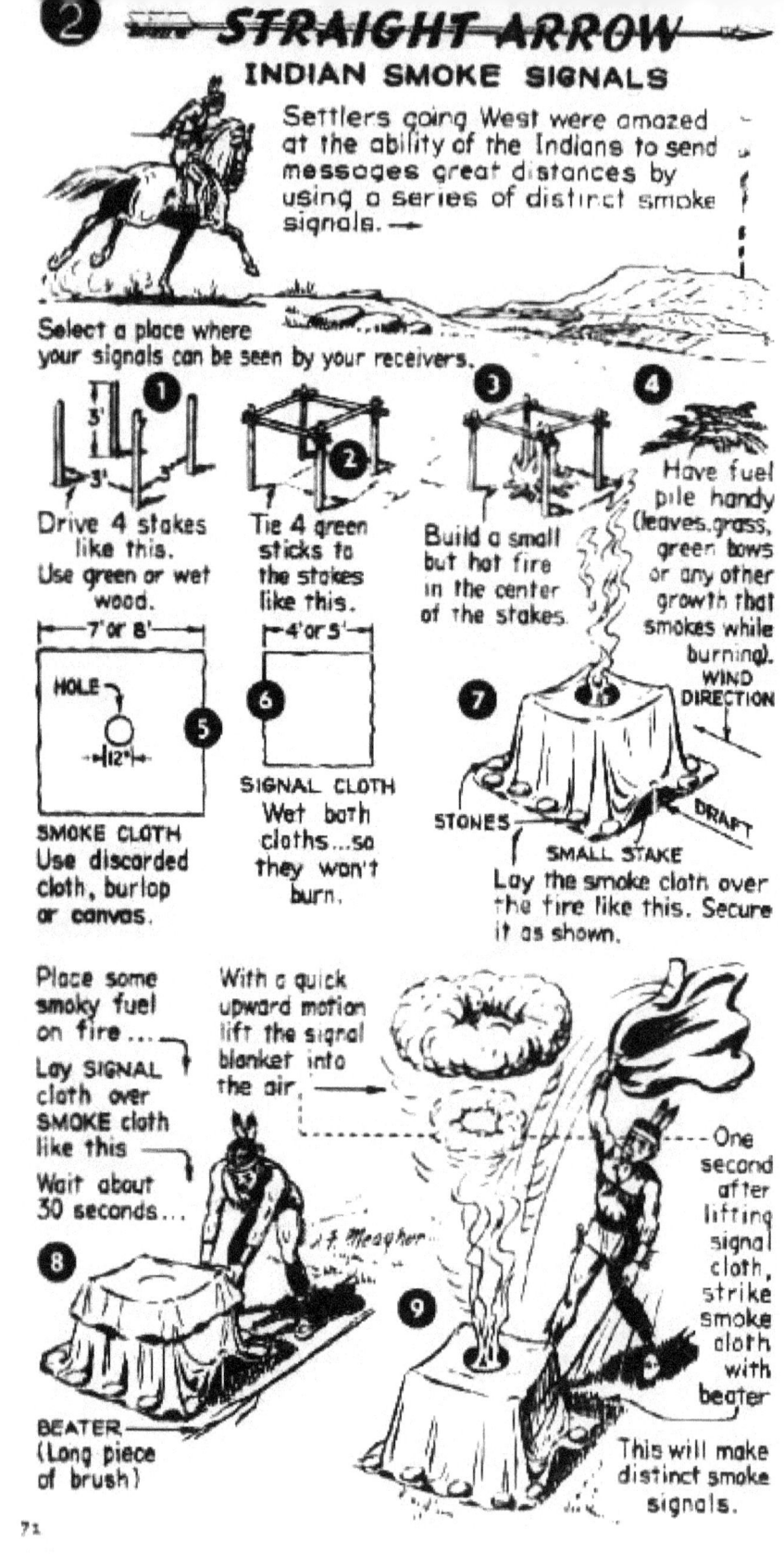

"THE CAVE OF GOLD"

(How Steve Adams became Straight Arrow)

Steve Adams, trailing the beautiful palomino he had been stalking for months, heard shots. He saw a lone rider pursued by outlaws. Turning from his task, Steve went to the stranger's aid. The two pulled away but were being hemmed in when suddenly the palomino appeared. Looking back at them, the great, golden horse trotted toward some bushes, and Steve, carrying his wounded friend, followed the stallion into a hidden valley and a secret cave ... a cave of Gold!

There the stranger, Packy McCloud, told him his pursuers had been stirring up the Indians and making trouble between them and the white settlers. And then Packy told of an old Indian legend. It said that some day a mysterious Indian would come ... taller and stronger and braver than any other who rode the plains. The legend went on, "When this great warrior was born, a gold arrowhead was hung around his neck. And he was called Straight Arrow. He will ride a golden horse, and shoot golden arrows. He alone will save the Indian tribes." It was then that Steve showed Packy a golden arrowhead hanging about his own neck. For he had been born an Indian — found and brought up by white ranchers. And when he was found, a golden arrow was hanging about his neck. "Then you're Straight Arrow!" exclaimed Packy.

Later in the cave, Steve found a golden bow and arrows, beautiful Comanche garments, and war paint. Soon, out burst the great golden palomino, Fury! Riding bareback, clad in Indian garb, came Straight Arrow on the trail of justice! And through the dusk like the crack of doom, rang this war cry, "Kaneewah, Fury!"

For the first of many thrilling times — Steve Adams, the Straight Arrow of legend, was riding from his secret cave on the trail of justice!

www.ingramcontent.com/pod-product-compliance
Lightning Source LLC
Chambersburg PA
CBHW031219090426
42736CB00009B/984